# SANTA FE FANTASY

# SANTA FE FANTASY

## QUEST FOR THE GOLDEN CITY

*by* ELMO BACA

*Foreword by Greer Garson*

CLEAR LIGHT PUBLISHERS
SANTA FE

Clear Light Publishers
823 Don Diego
Santa Fe, New Mexico 87501

LIBRARY OF CONGRESS CATALOGING-IN-PUBLICATION DATA
Baca, Elmo.
    Santa Fe fantasy: the quest for the golden city / Elmo Baca.
        p.  cm.
    Includes bibliographical references.
    ISBN  0-940666-14-6: $34.95
    1. Santa Fe (N.M.) —History.  2. Santa Fe (N. M.)—
Pictorial works.  I. Title
F 804.S257B33 1992
978.9'56—dc20                                        92-16121
                                                     CIP

First Edition
1 0 9 8 7 6 5 4 3 2 1

COVER: *Santa Fe Fantasy*, gouache on paper, © by Douglas Johnson.
Each window in Douglas Johnson's painting illustrates a different aspect
of "Santa Fe fantasy." Clockwise from the top:  Kiva Art of the Ancient
Ones; Spiritual Fantasy; The Modern Southwest; The Magical Land-
scape; Coronado, Fray Marcos de Niza, and Esteban; The Golden City.
Center windows—on right, Native Traders; on left, Zuñi Shalako
Ceremony. Inserts at the beginning of chapters are details from this
painting. (Courtesy the Gerald Peters Gallery, Santa Fe)

Dedicated to My Parents and Our Families:
The Bacas, Padillas, Jimenezes, and Sanchezes.

# CONTENTS

# FOREWORD

For many lucky years I have called New Mexico home. Inevitably this means that whenever I am anywhere else, its mysterious magic so haunts me that I long for the day when I leave the rush and tensions of the great teeming cities and return to the old ranch in the Pecos Valley, seven thousand feet up in the Sangre de Cristo Mountains. There the air is pure, and to breathe it is an exhilaration. The water is delicious, the sky unbelievably high and wide and of a deep, almost palpable blue.

One wakens in the shining spacious mornings feeling ten years old, and life is an adventure again. The remembered silence and the pleasant country sounds refresh the wearied spirit. Vision stretches gratefully to the far distant horizons. How good to see the great peaks and mesas, the fantastic towering rocks again, and the two-thousand-year-old pueblo ruins silhouetted against the spectacular sunsets.

How fair is our valley. Pine and piñon cover the red adobe land, and in the fall the aspens and cottonwoods along the Pecos River burn bright gold. In winter the forests are a white wonderland of Christmas trees. All year round the nights are crisp and cool, and the stars, startlingly brilliant, float in amethyst space and seem to bring heaven nearer to earth. If ever mortals could hear the music of the spheres, it would be in New Mexico.

For more than thirty-five years my late hus-band, Buddy, and I shared a busy life at Forked Lightning Ranch, with the thriving herd of Santa Gertrudis on the range and the constant flow of guests at the old hacienda. Here as everywhere the human element is part of the fascination. Our friends and fellow workers included Indian craftsmen, neighbors of Spanish descent from Pecos and other villages nearby, and pioneer westerners—merchants, cowboys, miners, sportsmen, ranchers, archaeologists, artists, and writers—a richly varied family bringing all the drama and romance of New Mexico's colorful past into its exciting present.

Where else in this world can you find such wide-ranging contrasts of ancient and modern? Prehistoric remains and nuclear laboratories; centuries-old Indian pueblos and modern luxury hotels; tribal ceremonials at Gallup, alfresco opera at Santa Fe; Spanish *santeros* and secret Penitentes in the mountains, the nation's most advanced space medicine center in Albuquerque; horse-drawn wagons on the country roads, air-conditioned buses and crack trains on the new railways; sleepy-hollow hidden villages, boomtowns in the uranium, oil, and gas fields; ageless caverns, mysterious rocks, and relics from the first furnace of creation.

Possibly the march of progress is more strikingly noticeable here in this ancient territory than elsewhere in the States. Romantics, of course, deplore the parking meters in the plaza at Santa Fe. (Me too . . . I even resent the automobiles!) They sigh to see the backyard hens and the family cow disappear in favor of the deep-freeze instant goodies at the updated country store. But some traditions stand firm. I doubt that factory-cooked pinto beans, tamales, tacos, or chile will ever displace the homemade kind. And although the lovely Mexican and Navajo costumes have to compete with drip-dry garments and blue jeans, they are still proudly worn by old and young. Junk jewelry glitters in the dime-stores and factory-made souvenirs in tourist shops, but they will never oust the treasured silver and turquoise, the handcrafted leather and pottery. The Indian languages are still in use, and Spanish is everywhere current and familiar.

When I moved here from the bright lights and glitter of Hollywood, I was determined to become a real part of the community: considering New Mexico's breathtaking charm and endearing willingness to embrace outsiders, it was an easy task. Through those wonderful years Buddy and I joined our neighbors in celebrating the annual Fiesta, lighting banks of *farolitos* at Christmas time, attending the many Indian festivals and dances, listening to the wonderful Santa Fe Opera under the stars.

To give a token back to this land we loved so much, we had the opportunity to support the various arts organizations in Santa Fe, St. Vincent's Hospital, and one of our favorite charities, the College of Santa Fe, which recently opened its Greer Garson Communication Center and Studios. We also had the pleasure of deeding a large portion of our ranch to the National Parks Service, so that visitors can now tour and appreciate the Pueblo monuments that have always given us a deep sense of serenity and a profound respect for the past.

Over the years I have seen many changes here—but change is characteristic of New Mexicans: they seem to know how to combine the best of old and new in a happy compromise. All around the countryside, for example, the small neat adobe house keeps its *horno* (oven), its well and animals, but nonchalantly sports a TV satellite dish on the roof and a pickup truck at the ol' hitching post.

Most important of all, the land itself changes not. Timeless, remote, and vast, it has absorbed all invaders from mastodons to missiles. Its beauty and power have inspired the artist, the writer, and the mystic. The magic can hardly be communicated, but this rich anthology gives you, Dear Reader, a vivid glimpse of the Land of Enchantment.

It is an honor to write the Foreword. I only wish I had the skill to express my thoughts and dreams and wonder, but it is hard to speak of one's religion, or of one's love. And there is something of both in my feeling for New Mexico.

Greer Garson
Forked Lightening Ranch
Pecos, New Mexico
February 1994

1. *(Below) A restored kiva at Pecos National Monument allows visitors to experience the sacred and mystical qualities of the subterranean ceremonial chamber. (Photograph by Marcia Keegan)*

2. *(Opposite page) The landscape of New Mexico is believed to possess intangible qualities which produce wonder, creative inspiration, and rapture. (Photograph by the author)*

# INTRODUCTION

The quest for a city of gold has kindled the imagination, daring, and greed of humankind for centuries. Fantastic cities and places have dotted the maps of continents and inspired legends and literature, from Plato's Atlantis to Saint Brendan's Island to the elusive kingdom of El Dorado, the "gilded one," an Indian chieftain whose body was covered with mud and sprayed with gold dust and who dived into a lake to wash off the gold every year to please the gods.

Today, we may laugh at the fantasies that drew early adventurers to make strange and dangerous voyages in search of an earthly paradise. However, one American city holds some of the allure of the fabled golden cities, having attracted explorers over the years with its combined promise of beauty, riches, and transcendent experience. For nearly four centuries, Santa Fe, New Mexico, has held a unique position among the world's cities. As the cultural, political, and spiritual capital of the American Southwest since 1610, Santa Fe continues to fulfill its destiny as the meeting ground of diverse peoples and several universes of ideas.

Today, the appeal of Santa Fe for the postmodern global citizen is complex, a combination of various forces that have developed over a long period of time. For many, Santa Fe's status as a Native American cultural mecca is at the core of the city's mystique. An appreciation of present-day Indian culture combines with a fascination with the past—with the mystery that surrounds petroglyph art and the stone ruins of ancestral civilizations.

Since its founding, Santa Fe has provided a stage for the encounter of the European cultures of Spain and Old Mexico and the powerful culture of the Native American peoples of the western frontier. With the blazing of the Santa Fe Trail in 1821, the relentless colonization of New Mexico and the Southwest by the United States commenced. By 1900, Santa Fe had already achieved a unique character and appearance, a blend of Spanish, Mexican, Indian, and North American influences.

New Mexico's Hispanic culture still boasts European qualities that many people find fascinating. Beginning shortly after Hernán Cortés's conquest of Mexico in 1521–1522, and drawn by the astonishing legend of the Seven Cities of Gold, Spanish colonists settled in the region. New Mexico's Hispanic culture is unlike any other in the world. Devout Catholicism, unique folk art forms, and well-preserved cultural traditions, such as special types of architecture and cuisine, endow New Mexico with haunting echoes of sixteenth-century Spain.

For many years during the Spanish colonial period, the "imagined" treasures of Santa Fe produced powerful fantasies in the minds of many Missouri traders. The Santa Fe Trail enabled scores of clever businessmen to create

*3. (Opposite page)* NASTURTIUMS, *casein, by Douglas Johnson. The skies in Johnson's tiny gem-like paintings are spiritual and emotional presences, here bloodred and fraught with dangerous foreboding, alternating with aquamarine, promising joy. An all-knowing bird gazes back at the viewer as if from lost worlds, guarding the secrets of pre-conquest glories. Johnson's is a romantic vision of North America before strange ships arrived from beyond the eastern horizon. (Courtesy the Gerald Peters Gallery, Santa Fe)*

vast fortunes not from gold but by exploiting the lucrative trade between the New Mexican and American frontiers, of which Santa Fe was the commercial hub. Santa Fe still boasts of its status as one of the world's great shopping and trading cities, a place where one-of-a-kind treasures are regularly bought and sold.

In the twentieth century, the discovery of Santa Fe by a score of talented artists and writers produced a series of cultural rebirths, which have firmly established the City of the Holy Faith as one of the leading art centers in North America. Some of the legendary artists who spent time in northern New Mexico, including D. H. Lawrence, Ansel Adams, and Georgia O' Keeffe, have ascribed almost mystical qualities to the creative spirit.

Just a young man of twenty-five in 1927, Ansel Adams described the "sky city" of Ácoma as "the most remarkable spot I ever expect to see. . . . An Indian village of great antiquity set on a lofty mesa in a wild desert landscape . . . impossible to tell of the beauty of the place and the effect of the color—the cream rocks and earth, the green-blue desert and the brilliant reds and yellows and blacks of the Indian costumes."

Today, New Mexico continues to produce superb, visionary artists whose works interpret the vast and profound themes of the Southwest. The long and sustained building tradition of adobe architecture in New Mexico has blessed Santa Fe with remarkable structures, giving the city a distinctive and storybook quality.

As the adobe mecca in the high desert of the southwestern United States, Santa Fe continues to provide a romantic vision of the western frontier, a vision perpetuated by Hollywood movies, television advertising, and Madison Avenue fashion campaigns. Its legendary ethereal qualities of pure light and air, coupled with the mysticism and mystery of Indian ceremonies still practiced, produce a subtle, hypnotic attraction.

Although seemingly a recent development, Santa Fe's unquestioned reputation as a New

Age spiritual center has deep historical roots in centuries-old religious ceremonialism and faith. For some, the land itself harbors great sacred power and healing properties. Clearly, many people are drawn to Santa Fe and its environs for transcendental reasons. Here, perhaps, is a bridge from the modern Fourth World of the southwestern Native American cosmos to dimensions beyond.

And so in many ways, on many levels, Santa Fe is a golden city, perhaps the modern-day Quivira—the fabled golden empire that Francisco Vásquez de Coronado and his conquistadors vainly sought in Kansas four and a half centuries ago. Now the ancient adobe capital is a manifestation of the dreams of countless explorers and adventurers, capitalists and visionaries, dancers and poets, buckaroos and urban exiles, each with his or her own Santa Fe fantasy.

4. (Below) UXMAL, casein on paper, by Douglas Johnson. The cultural roots of New Mexico are depicted in Johnson's vision at their zenith; Pueblo and Mayan cities are restored to their rightful grandeur. The success of Johnson's vision emanates from the artist's remarkable attention to detail—in buildings, landscape, costume, and artistic patterns. (Courtesy the Gerald Peters Gallery, Santa Fe)

5. (Opposite page) Hyde Park aspens. Acres of golden aspen trees blanket the Sangre de Cristo Mountains above Santa Fe each autumn. (Photograph by Marcia Keegan)

# THE FIRST PEOPLE

In his classic work *Book of the Hopi* *
Frank Waters tells the story of the emergence of "the People" into four successive worlds. The Creator was said to have destroyed each of the first three worlds when human beings forgot their duties and abused the powers and gifts the Creator had bestowed upon them. Waters speaks of how those who had followed the Creator's teachings survived each destruction and emerged safely in the next world. The Third World was destroyed, as in the biblical story, by flood.

When the clans emerged in this present Fourth World, they were aided by spiritual beings such as the Spider Woman and Kokopelli, the humpbacked flute player, during the long years of migration in search of the homelands they were destined to occupy. The homeland of the clans who would remain in the Southwest was the region now called the Four Corners, where the borders of Arizona, Utah, Colorado, and New Mexico meet. It is the cradle of the most ancient civilizations of the Southwest.

## Homeland of the Ancient Ones

As the clans passed from legend into history, their stories preserved the memory of their migrations to their sacred homeland. The Hopis believe that their ancestors landed ashore near what is now Central America during their journey of emergence into the Fourth World.

Testifying to the reality of their legends, Kokopelli's image is carved on rocks spread over both continents of the Western Hemisphere. Kokopelli first made his appearance on rocks in the Four Corners area about A.D. 600. Archaeologists tell us that the Hopi and other Pueblo people they call the Anasazi** (also referred to as the "Ancient Ones") settled in the Four Corners area and built cities out of rock and mud about A. D. 1000.

Kokopelli may be a long-lost link between the present-day Pueblo peoples and the hidden past of such mysterious settlements as the cities

*Frank Waters, *Book of the Hopi* (New York: Viking Press, 1963).

** The commonly used term *Anasazi* is a Navajo word that translates roughly as "the enemies of my ancestors" and has no relation to the language of the Hopi and Pueblo people themselves.

6. (Opposite page) Pueblo Bonito with a kiva in the background, Chaco Canyon. Sacred Chaco Canyon still guards its secrets after nearly a millennium. Precise masonry and urban design are a lasting tribute to the creators of this complex ceremonial center. (Photograph by Marcia Keegan)

of Chaco Canyon and Mesa Verde, and the glorious Mesoamerican world that existed before the New World was encountered by European explorers.

Members of the Hopi Flute Clan wear brightly colored parrot and macaw feathers and sea shells during ceremonials to invoke the warm, life-giving rains of summer. The discovery of parrot feathers and sea shells (and also copper bells) in some ancient ruins near the Four Corners area by archaeologists produced dramatic evidence that trade existed in ancient times between peoples of the Southwest and Mexico. Among the artifacts discovered at Chaco Canyon, the skeletons of fourteen macaws were found in one room. Feathers from other tropical birds were also found.

From about A.D. 500 onward, the Ancient Ones evolved from a primitive agricultural society to one capable of remarkable architectural and engineering feats, most notably those at Chaco Canyon in northwestern New Mexico. The twelve separate rock and adobe pueblos in close proximity in the Chaco Wash represented the heart of a complex and far-flung cultural empire, though its exact nature is still under debate.

As a counterpoint, Mesa Verde, in southwestern Colorado, required a different, organic response to its huge cliff-side caverns—which the Ancient Ones masterfully provided. Chaco Canyon and Mesa Verde represent the most sophisticated and substantial Native American archaeological sites within the United States, the

7. *Rock drawings near Zuñi. Origin symbols, a humpbacked flute player (Kokopelli), mythological creatures, and various animals help tell the story of emergence at this rock outcropping near Zuñi. (Photograph by the author)*

proving ground for many of America's leading archaeologists in the early twentieth century.

As part of the research for his classic *Book of the Hopi*, author Frank Waters and two Hopi colleagues went to Chaco Canyon more than thirty years ago. There they discovered hidden stone shrines, believed to be the markers of ancient racecourses linking Chaco Canyon and the Sun Temple at Mesa Verde in southwestern Colorado, a journey of three or four days by foot.

It is theorized that ceremonial footraces were staged along these tracks by the Flute Clan at Chaco Canyon, with a jar of sacred water awarded to the winning runner. This jar would bring rains to the fields of the victor's family. Over the years, more and more clans began competing for water, with the result that it became an ever rarer commodity, forcing the Flute Clan and the other clans, and the inhabitants of the cities of Chaco Canyon and Mesa Verde, to migrate in search of it.

Recent archaeological evidence seems to support the possibility of a racecourse between Chaco Canyon and Mesa Verde. Aerial photography has helped identify a far-flung network of roads emanating from Chaco Canyon in all directions. Scholars agree that Chaco Canyon functioned as a ceremonial center for the Ancient Ones. However, many mysteries, including the purpose of various outlying ruins and structures, still remain to be solved.

A severe drought beginning in A.D. 1276, as well as other difficulties, apparently compelled the Ancient Ones to abandon their homeland. The nearby Rio Grande watershed in the east, nourished by the runoff from the Sangre de Cristo Mountains, provided ideal refuge for many of the clans, though the Hopis, Zuñis, Lagunas, and Ácomas stayed in the west.

The mass exodus from the Four Corners region left a vacuum, which the wandering Navajos, newcomers from the north, quickly filled. Within a few generations they domi-

nated the region formerly occupied by the Ancient Ones, even inhabiting their old sites, such as the cliff and river houses at Canyon de Chelly. In time, the Navajos learned agriculture and weaving from the descendants of the Ancient Ones and managed somehow to eke out an existence in the harsh environment of the high desert.

Though the Ancient Ones crafted pottery and buildings of amazing quality, they left no writing other than petroglyphs and kiva murals to indicate their history and origin. It is believed, however, that their folklore, oral history, and ceremonialism are still perpetuated by their descendants, the modern Pueblo tribes.

Today, as more and more people migrate to New Mexico and the Southwest, water will again become a precious commodity. Kokopelli will again be called upon to produce the warm summer rains that sustain life in the arid homeland of the Ancient Ones. And his flute will produce the hauntingly beautiful melodies that soothe and mesmerize, serenading the mesas and sierras and pricking the ears of the trickster Coyote with secrets of the ancestors.

8. (Left) Mesa Verde Cliff Palace. In contrast to the geometric design of the Chaco Canyon pueblos, Mesa Verde's villages are masterpieces of organic architecture. Here, landscape and solar orientation were the primary guidelines for the builders. (Photograph by the author)

9. (Right) Doorways at Chaco Canyon. The precision of construction details within Chaco Canyon's Pueblo Bonito continues to amaze visitors and scholars alike. (Photograph by the author)

## Foreigners Invade the Homeland

Had not the Spanish fantasy of seven golden cities compelled Coronado to explore the American Southwest, the Pueblo, Navajo, and Apache tribes of New Mexico would have coexisted in relative isolation for perhaps another two centuries. Beginning with the Spanish colonization of the region in 1598, life altered dramatically for the Pueblo peoples, and the balance of power that had existed for generations among the various tribes was shattered.

In the seventeenth century, the Spaniards unleased a force they ultimately could not control—the horse. This marvelous new animal gave power and mobility to the Navajos and Apaches and later to the Comanches and other Indians from the southern plains, who plundered Spanish colonists and Pueblos alike, stealing livestock and even women and children.

Although the Spanish, with their horses and well-armed soldiers, had allied themselves with the Pueblos for mutual defense against the marauding tribes, the Pueblos rose in 1680 in a well-organized revolt. The Spanish government collapsed, and the Spaniards—officials, soldiers, settlers, and priests—fled south to Mexico. There were two principal causes of the revolt: the brutal enforcement of a repressive economic system, which exacted slave labor and a heavy burden of tithes, and the zealous efforts of the Catholic Church to suppress native religious beliefs and practices.

The Spanish returned twelve years later. Resistance by the Pueblos continued until 1696, but within a short time all of the Pueblo leaders had formed alliances with the Spanish colonists in order to defend their villages and farms against raiding nomadic Indians. Despite Spanish military campaigns and the Pueblo alliances, however, these intrepid Indian horsemen roamed the Southwest at will until the U.S. Army arrived about 1850.

The Pueblo tribes persevered through the long Spanish colonial years, enduring both European cultural domination and their enemies on horseback. But they paid a heavy price. Disease, warfare, persecution, and famine reduced their numbers greatly. An estimated population of about 50,000 Pueblo people at the time of first contact with the Europeans was reduced to between 16,000 and 30,000 by 1675.

Although the Spanish continued to force Roman Catholicism on the native population, the Pueblos retained their own religious ceremonies. Down to the present day they continue to practice the most sacred aspects of their religion in secret and perform ritual dances for feast days, solstices, and rain, while at the same time observing Catholic feast days and other Christian holidays.

The brief period of Mexican rule (1821–1848) saw little change in the Native American way of life, with the exception of the pioneering of the Santa Fe Trail. Soon "foreign" goods—textiles, tools, coins, and other sundry items—were to have an impact on their art and culture.

The American annexation of Mexico's northern territories, including Texas, New Mexico, and California, in 1848 produced disastrous consequences for the resident Native American

10. *Modern Zuñi rock paintings. Contemporary versions of Zuñi kachinas are painted on walls of a remote rock cave near Zuñi Pueblo. These images are about fifty years old. (Photograph by the author)*

tribes. The nomadic tribes, notably the Navajo, Apache, and Comanche, were systematically hunted down and exiled to harsh reservations.

Starved into submission by the U.S. Army under the command of Colonel Kit Carson in 1864, the Navajos endured the "Long Walk" —a trek of over 300 miles from their stronghold in Canyon de Chelly east to a virtual concentration camp at Bosque Redondo. Soldiers also burned the cherished and sacred fruit orchards of the Navajos, causing a deep wound that still haunts the Navajo psyche.

But New Mexico's indigenous peoples quietly and defiantly nurtured themselves, their spirit, their faith, and their culture through the worst of times, emerging as triumphant survivors into the new world of the twentieth century.

## Modern Native American Culture in the Southwest

By 1900, almost all of the Native American peoples had been decimated. The Pueblos have survived with perhaps the least damage. In part their survival may be due to their stable architecture and culture, which made them less frequent targets of military action. The Navajos negotiated a treaty with the U.S. government that allowed them to return home in 1868, and the Mescalero Apaches were subsequently granted their own reservation.

By 1915, artists and intellectuals in America and Europe began to appreciate the integrity and beauty of America's native cultures. In the United States, artists such as Frederic Remington and Charles M. Russell forged a romantic, cinematic vision of the western frontier, fusing the rich colors of the West with a dramatic sense of design, often depicting Americans and Native Americans in a fierce struggle for survival against nature or one another. Edward Curtis, Adam Clark Vroman, and other frontier photographers produced classic and elegant pictures of southwestern Indians. Many of these artists and photographers believed they were capturing the last glimmer of life of a dying people.

But the past hundred years have witnessed a remarkable resurgence and ultimate triumph of southwestern Indian culture. The nineteen Pueblo tribes of New Mexico have weathered

*11. (Opposite) Zuñi kachina doll. Kachina dolls were originally crafted to instruct children about the gods. (Photograph by Marcia Keegan)*

*12. (Below) Laguna Pueblo. Along with its sister pueblo of Ácoma, Laguna represents a classic example of historic Pueblo architecture, built after the exodus from the Four Corners area in the late thirteenth century. Both Laguna and Ácoma pueblos are remarkably preserved. At the center is Laguna's mission church of San José. (Photograph by the author)*

economic hardships and political pressures, including the federal government's attempts to terminate tribal status and force assimilation of Native Americans throughout the country. For a time it seemed that many aspects of Pueblo culture would die out as the elders passed on, but renewed interest among Pueblo people of all ages has spurred a major cultural revival. Efforts to preserve and transmit the five tribal languages of New Mexico have been stepped up. Every year more people participate in the ancient deer, eagle, buffalo, and corn dances, and care is taken to protect the most sacred rituals from curious tourists.

The artistic revival is expressed in a reaffirmed commitment to learning traditional crafts and expanding creative boundaries. Dazzling works of Navajo weaving and jewelry; Pueblo pottery, jewelry, painting, and sculpture; and Apache basketmaking now dominate western art markets and rank among the finest indigenous American art being produced.

Within the past few decades, the ascendancy of Santa Fe as an art market (it is the nation's third largest) has helped skyrocket the careers of numerous Native American artists who live in or near Santa Fe. In addition, types of native artisanship formerly considered handicrafts are now regarded as fine art. The finest pottery, weaving, jewelry, and baskets are produced as art objects and not merely for utilitarian purposes.

This change in status has produced a virtual renaissance in southwestern Indian arts in the past twenty years, as artists have juxtaposed traditional media in innovative ways. Pottery, turquoise, silver, and other materials such as fur, bone, feathers, and paint have been creatively combined and worked. Pottery can be etched, painted, and inlaid with precious materials; alabaster can be sculpted; and masks can be airbrushed. After fifteen hundred years of tradition and development, the art of the native southwestern peoples is perhaps only now showing evidence of its full potential, a true testament to the resourcefulness and genius of its creators.

Santa Fe has become the preeminent market and forum for Native American art in the Western Hemisphere, perhaps in the world. Its annual Indian Market, the second largest outdoor market in the world, is held in August. It attracts close to 100,000 people, many of them serious collectors or purchasers for major galleries throughout the United States. The sheer abundance of art galleries impresses first-time visitors and longtime residents alike.

*13. (Left) Deer Dance at San Ildefonso Pueblo. (Photograph by Marcia Keegan)*

*14. (Below) Hopi basket, yucca fiber and natural pigments, by Madeline Lampson. Lampson's basket is unusual for its relatively large size and olla form. This basket won the Best of Show prize at Gallup's Intertribal Indian Ceremonial Exhibition. (Photograph by Lisa Wallace, Light Language Studio; courtesy Intertribal Indian Ceremonial Association, Gallup)*

For many Native American artists, Santa Fe is still a golden city. Success in the ancient New Mexican capital can lead to sales and commissions from New York, Hollywood, and the capitals of Europe. But the best artists know that the spiritual rewards of creativity are the most lasting.

Today, 56,000 Pueblo people thrive in nineteen pueblos and as many as 250,000 Navajos live in the dynamic region of northern and northwestern New Mexico. In the Old West, only Santa Fe can still claim to be an Indian capital, and though commercial influences are sometimes unfortunate, its status as a city of opportunity for Native Americans is secure and growing.

*15. Historical cross necklaces. The extra crossbar on a Navajo cross symbolizes the life line. This distinctive symbol is also a holy sign encouraging Navajo people to "walk in harmony." (Photograph by Eric Swanson; courtesy Dewey Gallery, Santa Fe)*

*16. Navajo ketoh. This man's large bracelet, or ketoh, is a stylized interpretation of a traditional bow guard, worn on the lower arm to protect from bowstring burns and to help steady the archer's aim. (Photograph by Eric Swanson; courtesy Dewey Gallery, Santa Fe)*

*17. (Lower right) Hopi olla, ceramic and paint, by James Nampeyo. This classic Hopi pot bears the unmistakable influence of James's famed ancestor Nampeyo in the scroll and medallion designs. (Photograph by Lisa Wallace, Light Language Studio, Gallup; courtesy Intertribal Indian Ceremonial Association, Gallup)*

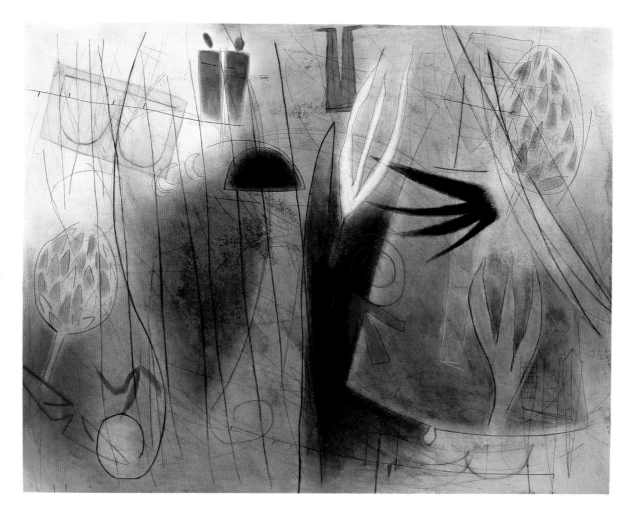

18. MAN AND WOMAN, *paper on canvas with oil, by Emmi Whitehorse. Born in Crownpoint, New Mexico, Navajo artist Emmi Whitehorse has created a unique visual language incorporating primal subconscious symbols which reflect her Native American upbringing and also the universal dreamscape of the human psyche. Whitehorse achieves a wonderful lustrous patina in her works by rubbing pigments into the paper fiber. (Courtesy LewAllen Gallery, Santa Fe)*

19. WALTER CARMON, *woodblock, by T. C. Cannon. Cannon's meteoric rise to the top of the art world and early tragic death are the stuff of legend. In his brief career, Cannon created an impressive body of work showing an easy mastery of color and many visual media. His "pop" images of Native Americans combine humor with biting sarcasm. (Courtesy Zaplin-Lampert Gallery, Santa Fe)*

20. *(Opposite page)* KACHINA SYMBOL-ISM, *acrylic on canvas, by Dan Namingha. Hopi artist Dan Namingha has created a bold contemporary style incorporating fluid, painterly technique with symbolic, expressionistic imagery. He includes references to the Morning Star Kachina and the Zuñi Jemez Kachina in this recent composition. (Courtesy Niman Fine Art, Santa Fe)*

# THE SPANISH QUEST

L egends of golden cities have lured explorers on impossible quests since ancient times. Greek writers of antiquity, such as the philosopher Plato and the epic poet          Homer, both described a legendary land where "the earth gave men an abundance of fruits which grew on trees and shrubs unbidden," a place where private property was unknown and people lived in harmony and happiness.

## The Quest for the Seven Cities of Gold

To the earliest sailors of the Mediterranean Sea, the Pillars of Hercules, the great rock cliffs of the Straits of Gibraltar, were the threshold to the unknown. Beyond the Pillars of Hercules beckoned a vast sea, fraught with danger but perhaps yielding riches or an earthly paradise. Plato speculated that there, in the Western Sea, lay the amazing civilization of Atlantis and also the fabulously wealthy Isles of Antilia. If only seaworthy vessels and brave sailors with stout hearts could conquer the demons of the unknown, Atlantis and Antilia could perhaps be found.

With the rise of Christianity, biblical legends and stories continued to fascinate scholars and writers concerned with fantastic places. The Garden of Eden was believed to exist as a place on earth, and the pursuit of its discovery was considered a noble quest, worthy of the

pious and pure-hearted.

Monks of the Middle Ages gained fame and notoriety for their adventures in search of the Garden of Eden. Somewhere beyond lands inhabited by dog-headed men, pygmies, and serpents, surrounded by a fiery wall, lay the Garden of Eden.

The Irish monk Saint Brendan (A.D. 484–578) believed that paradise was somewhere in the Atlantic Ocean. Off to the west he sailed, surviving harrowing trials and tribulations, before discovering a beautiful island of unsurpassed beauty. "Saint Brendan's Island" joined

*21. (Opposite page)* THE BURIAL OF COUNT ORGAZ, *1586, by El Greco. El Greco's monumental painting of the burial of Count Orgaz in 1323 is generally considered one of the masterpieces of Spain's golden age. Count Orgaz was a virtuous nobleman who served the poor and needy of Toledo. Saint Augustine and Saint Stephen, depicted in bishop's garments, are said to have appeared miraculously at the funeral. The count's soul is welcomed into heaven in the center of the picture by a pantheon of saints and angels. Below are gathered many nobles of Spanish society. El Greco includes a self-portrait—seventh figure from left, standing. (Saint Tome's Church, Toledo, Spain)*

Atlantis and Antilia in the mythical pantheon, a destination vainly pursued by explorers until it disappeared from maps in 1759.

Stories of scores of mythic places and creatures abounded during the Middle Ages. Among the more remarkable legends, with origins as early as the Greek historian Herodotus (485–425 B.C.), was that of the Amazon women, fierce female warriors who cut off their left breasts in order to use bows and arrows.

The Moorish invasion of the Iberian peninsula in A.D. 711 enhanced the ancient legend of the Isles of Antilia. Seven Portuguese bishops fleeing before the advancing armies of Islam hastily boarded ships and set sail into the Western Sea. The bishops were blown off course by a terrible North Atlantic storm and were shipwrecked on unknown islands. According to legend, each of the seven bishops had discovered his own island, each with its own capital city, each city guarding a secret cache of incredible riches from unknown continents. Unable to sail back to the mainland, the bishops were lost to memory and history but roamed the strange landscape of the European imagination for centuries.

The Seven Cities of Antilia were thought to exist by the great Portuguese and Spanish mariners, who dramatically expanded knowledge of the world in the fourteenth, fifteenth, and sixteenth centuries. Early maps of the New World, not long after Columbus's discovery, still displayed the Seven Cities of Antilia floating somewhere in the middle of the Atlantic Ocean.

During the crusades, while Spain was still dominated by the Moors, the legend of Prester John swept through Christendom. Prester John was said to reign over an immensely wealthy empire located in the "Western Indies." Descended from the race of the Three Wise Men, Prester John was believed to have conquered the Muslims in his own kingdom by virtue of his superior wisdom, faith in God, and wealth.

About A.D. 1165, a mysterious letter was delivered to the Byzantine emperor of Rome, Em-

manuel I, and also to the king of France. The letter was from Prester John himself, pledging his assistance in defense of the Holy Land. Though a forgery, the letter was circulated throughout Europe, creating widespread speculation that the fabled Kingdom of the West existed. Prince Henry the Navigator of Portugal (A.D. 1394–1460), whose patronage of the bold Portuguese mariners was an essential prelude to the voyage of Columbus, sought in vain for the mythical Prester John.

Christian utopias such as Prester John's played an important role in the Spanish psyche. Perhaps the long domination of Christians by Muslims on the Iberian peninsula had encouraged compensating visions of rich and devoutly Catholic kingdoms.

As the overpowering zeal to expel the Muslim "infidels" from Spain grew in the fifteenth century, so did the appeal of romantic popular fiction describing the adventures of great soldiers and knights in armor. Royal orders of knights, sworn to defend the Crown and Church, existed in Spain for centuries during the long siege against Islam. After successfully expelling the last Muslims from Granada in 1492, a large class of professional soldiers, the conquistadors, were ready for new challenges.

The literary tradition of Spain during the Age of Discovery helps explain the motivation of the men and women who explored and settled much of North and South America. Popular romance novels of the era celebrated adventurous themes of conquest, discovery, exploration, and golden riches. Young Spanish men learned to be fearless, persistent, brave in battle, and domineering from these books.

*Amadis of Gaul*, a book published in 1508 by García-Rodríguez de Montalvo, described the adventures of a young prince adopted by the king of Scotland, who falls hopelessly in love with the king's daughter, the Princess Oriana. To win his bride, Amadis must perform several valorous works, surviving amazing adventures and tests of courage. *Amadis of Gaul* proved so successful that, anticipating the sequel, a dozen subsequent adventure books on Amadis were published and eagerly devoured by the Spanish public.

In the sixteenth century, books were very rare and expensive. Anything printed at that time was accepted as the virtual truth, and therefore the fictions, romances, and unbelievable adventures of heroes such as Amadis were treated as fact. A century later, a genius such as Cervantes was able to poke fun at the Spanish obsession with myth and adventure in his epic *Don Quixote*, but in 1508 the legends of *Amadis of Gaul* and of the Seven Cities of Antilia seemed very real.

The first reports from the New World, describing "Indian" cultures, great stretches of beautiful wilderness, strange new foods and animals, and other wonders found a welcoming audience in Spain. Within thirty years of Columbus's first voyage, Spaniards would hear stories of the conquest of a floating Aztec city by Hernán Cortés and the capture of the mountain empire of the Incas by Pizarro. Soon after the conquest of Mexico, as early as 1529, Nuño de Guzmán, governor of the northern Mexican province of Nueva Galicia, had heard stories from Indian scouts of seven rich northern cities. The Spaniards, eager to believe in another fabulously wealthy culture, equated the seven cities north of Mexico with the mythical Seven Cities of Antilia. The ancient European legend thus

took root in American soil. The Seven Cities of Gold prophesied so long ago seemed on the verge of being finally located.

While the European passion for gold was not the primary reason for Columbus's voyage to the unknown across the Western Sea, it certainly was an obsession of every sailor who made the hazardous journey after him.

Hernán Cortés's conquest of Mexico in 1521–1522, only three decades after the discovery of the New World, provided tangible proof of the existence of incredible wealth waiting to be found. Gold and silver for the king and souls for the Church were equally valued as prizes of conquest. Native American cultures were ignored, desecrated, and destroyed by the Europeans in their greedy fervor.

The Spanish conquest of Mexico was as harsh as it was complete. Priceless examples of Aztec and other pre-Columbian filigree gold jewelry were melted down into ingots for the minting of gold coins and pieces of eight; Hernán Cortés, Marqués del Valle, built his palace in Cuernavaca in 1524 atop a ruined Aztec temple, arrogantly recycling the stones for his own fortress.

The tragic and fateful conquest of the Aztec capital of Tenochtitlán seemed to validate every European dream of a golden city. In fact, Tenochtitlán *was* a golden city before Cortés and his followers destroyed it. Built upon Lake Tex-

23. Model of Tenochtitlán, Aztec imperial capital. Tenochtitlán, the magical capital city of the Aztecs, boasted 250,000 residents when it was first sighted by Cortés and his army in 1519. "When we saw all those cities and villages built in the water, and other great towns on dry land, and the straight and level causeway leading to Mexico, we were astounded," wrote Bernal Diaz in his eyewitness account, The Conquest of New Spain. "These great towns and temples and buildings rising from the water, all made of stone, seemed like an enchanted vision." The ceremonial complex seen here was dominated by the great Templo Mayor, a twin pyramid built to honor Huitzilopochtli (god of war) and Tlaloc (god of rain). (Museum of Anthropology, Mexico City, photograph by the author)

coco and joined to the mainland by causeways and canals, it boasted over 100,000 people and was the center of a vast empire. Great quantities of foodstuffs, pelts, armor, animals, body ornaments, and other items of value were paid yearly to the Aztec emperor by his subjects. Gold was considered just one treasure among many by the native Mexicans. Since gold could not be eaten, it was less valuable than cacao beans, which produced the rich *chocolatl* drink the emperor Montezuma craved. Still, Aztec craftsmen produced fantastic gold necklaces and earrings, masterfully combining the yellow metal with copper, silver, malachite, jade, and even iridescent quetzal feathers.

Beneath its twin snowcapped volcanoes, Popocatépetl and Iztaccíhuatl, the floating metropolis of Tenochtitlán made an awesome sight and was compared by Spanish chronicler Bernal Díaz del Castillo to Rome and Constantinople. If such a city could be subdued by only 200 armed soldiers, surely there were other cities and places to plunder.

## Cabeza de Vaca and Esteban

Meanwhile, another drama was being played out on the stage of world history. Alvar Nuñez Cabeza de Vaca was one of thousands of young Spaniards seeking his destiny on the new frontier after Cortés's conquest. A lieutenant under the command of a reckless redhead, one-eyed Panfilo Narvaez, Cabeza de Vaca was one of four survivors of a Spanish expedition that went dismally awry in 1528. After crossing much of western Florida on foot and failing to meet the fleet they expected to rescue them, the battered remnants of the expedition built crude barges and floated along the Gulf of Mexico until bad weather, thirst, and disease forced them ashore near present-day Galveston.

The other survivors were an African called Esteban, who became a legend himself, Captain Alfonso de Castillo, and Andrés Dorantes. Had these men drowned, the history of the Southwest, of the United States, and of Santa Fe would have been drastically altered.

Esteban possessed exceptional linguistic skills, which enabled his small party not only to survive but rise to cult status among the nomadic Native American tribes that roamed the plains of Texas. For a time, Cabeza de Vaca and the three others were slaves, but eventually they made a reputation among the native peoples

*24. (Left) Pre-Columbian filigree jewelry, gold. Goldsmiths in the Americas had achieved a remarkable quality of delicate filigree work and artistic expression before the Europeans arrived. Unfortunately, countless examples of this golden art were melted into coins and ingots for the king of Spain.*

*25. (Lower left) Man's head, stone, Aztec culture. Aztec and other Mesoamerican sculpture often featured remarkable portraiture qualities, as revealed in this sculpture of a man's head, complete with mustache and other facial adornments. (Photograph by the author, National Museum of Anthropology, Mexico City)*

*26. (Lower right) Merchant, stone, Aztec culture. Merchants, or pochteca, were highly regarded in Aztec culture. This sculpture may be a depiction of Yacatecuhtli, the patron god of merchants, carrying a bundle of sacred feathers for trade. (Photograph by the author, National Museum of Anthropology, Mexico City)*

27. SPANISH GREED, *fresco (detail), by Diego Rivera. Rivera's monumental frescos in the National Palace of Mexico depict the history of Mexico from a Mexican point of view. Here, Spain and its colonizers are depicted as greedy usurpers, destroying the glorious pre-Columbian native cultures of Mexico and shamelessly exploiting native labor and the wealth of the land. (National Palace, Mexico City, photograph by the author)*

they met by enacting miraculous "healing" ceremonies using their only remaining Spanish possessions—a few coins and forged metal objects—as magic charms.

For nearly eight years the small band of miracle workers crisscrossed the plains of Texas. Esteban's black skin and fluid tongue were taken to confirm his status as a "spiritual" being. Warriors and chiefs alike paid tribute to the healers, offering gifts such as precious feathers, jewelry, and other adornments—and sometimes traveling substantial distances to do so.

Cabeza de Vaca's company gradually drifted westward, occasionally staying with tribes for more than a year. As they approached the Pecos River in eastern New Mexico, visiting traders began referring to "rich" cities in the north, in a land called Cíbola, where the residents lived in fine houses, planted crops, and wore cloth garments. Could these be the fabled Seven Cities of Antilia?

Before Cabeza de Vaca's band could attempt to reach the wealthy northern lands, divine providence intervened. The Europeans were incredulous to see a Spanish horseshoe nail dangling from the necklace of one of the native emissaries. After what must have seemed like a lifetime lost in an endless wilderness, here was hope in the form of a piece of metal!

The shipwreck survivors followed their guides westward across southern New Mexico and into the unexplored frontier of northern Mexico. There they encountered Opata Indian traders who by their gestures indicated there were others like Cabeza de Vaca where they were going. Finally, with the help of their Opata friends, the only known survivors of the ill-fated Narvaez expedition of 1528 made it back to civilization in Mexico after an arduous adventure of eight years.

The Spanish authorities were just as amazed to see Cabeza de Vaca as he was to have found them. His incredible stories of life among the natives quickly spread, especially the native traders' tale of rich northern cities. By the time Cabeza de Vaca reached Mexico City, his fame had preceded him, and the Seven Cities of Gold loomed heavily on the northern horizon.

## Fray Marcos de Niza

Spanish Viceroy Antonio de Mendoza, while tantalized by the possibility of another lucrative conquest, acted cautiously and prudently. Before authorizing a major force to subdue the Seven Cities of Gold, he wished to verify their existence. For this task, he chose Fray Marcos de Niza, a sober and dedicated friar who had gained a reputation as an honest and fair public servant while working in Peru and Guatemala. Cabeza de Vaca had had his fill of adventure in the vast northern wasteland and declined to accompany Fray Marcos. But Esteban relished the chance to return to a land where he was considered magic incarnate. The viceroy granted his request to serve as a guide for Fray Marcos.

The small party of Fray Marcos, Father Onerato, Esteban, and several Indian allies departed from Culiacán in March 1539 and marched northward in search of the Seven Cities. Accompanying them were a group of Indian guides. Fray Marcos carried pieces of gold, pearls, and jewels so that the residents of the Seven Cities would be willing to receive them as guests. Esteban carried a magic healing gourd rattle he had acquired from his earlier adventures in Texas. After following the Sierra Madres and crossing into what is now central Arizona, the native guides indicated that the cities were nearby.

Fray Marcos's good judgment then failed him. Deciding to send Esteban ahead with a small contingent of guards, Fray Marcos instructed the Moor to send back a small, palm-size cross if modest communities were encountered. Larger crosses were to be sent back if true riches lay ahead. Fray Marcos would follow a few days behind.

Unknown to the Europeans, they were approaching a territory rich in culture but poor in gold. The homeland of the Ancient Ones encircled by the Colorado River and the Rio Grande was inhabited by an industrious and

civilized people who had lived there for at least a thousand years.

The de Niza party was in fact approaching the pueblos of the Zuñi tribe, which were nestled in a picturesque valley rimmed by dramatic striped sandstone bluffs, or mesas. Several different towns of rock and mud construction rose to several stories in height. But the walls were whitewashed with gypsum and not plated with silver.

The Zuñi pueblos had maintained extensive trading connections with several distant peoples, obtaining parrot feathers and copper bells from southern Mexico for ceremonial purposes, sea shells from western tribes for jewelry, and meat and hides from the Plains Indians. These latter were buffalo hunters who probably roamed the same country Esteban had left behind just a few years earlier.

From afar, the compact, picturesque pueblos were an impressive sight compared to the lodgings Esteban had seen on the Texas plains. Esteban's subsequent actions and fate are known to us only through legend and supposition, but they are significant because they led to the exploration and eventual settlement of the American Southwest.

To Esteban, the sight of the Zuñi pueblos meant fortune and fame. He did not hesitate to send a man-size cross to Fray Marcos indicating his enthusiasm. But the "magical" theatrics that served him so well in Texas spelled his doom in Zuñi. The rattle he sent as a talisman of his power may have angered the Zuñis, since they knew it to be a Plains Indian rattle, symbol of their traditional enemies.

Whatever the cause, Esteban and a few of his native assistants were killed by the Zuñis. Those who survived the attack found Fray Marcos a few days later and recounted the terrible story of Esteban's execution. Still wishing to fulfill his mission, Fray Marcos pushed on to a place that may have given him a distant view of Hawikuh, a large Zuñi pueblo. Fray Marcos wanted to believe the Seven Cities existed. The ferocity of the natives suggested they were protecting their great treasures. On that day, Fray Marcos saw many unusual things, and he was sure he was the first European to finally gaze upon the Seven Cities of myth and dream.

## Coronado's Expedition of 1540

When Fray Marcos and his devastated party returned to Mexico in June 1539, they reported to Don Francisco Vásquez de Coronado, who had just been appointed governor of Nueva Galicia the year before. The friar claimed that he had seen a city larger than Mexico City that was built up ten stories high and whose doorways boasted decorations of turquoise and precious jewels. He was certain that the cities of the north were hoarding stashes of gold. He called the region "Cíbola," which may have been a corruption of a Zuñi name.

Fray Marcos recounted the same fantastic tale before Viceroy Mendoza in Mexico City in

September. The viceroy's interest in the enchanted cities was now ablaze, but he still exercised prudence, sending another party of horsemen northward under the command of Melchior Díaz, a talented and able scout. Although some of the Indian tribes he visited in northern Mexico verified the existence of the northern cities, gold and riches were conspicuously absent from their stories. But for the viceroy, the die had

been cast. He could not afford for someone else to find the fabled cities.

Meanwhile, rumors of a new empire to be conquered swarmed throughout the countryside. Many bold men clamored for the royal commission to march on Cíbola, but Mendoza chose the twenty-nine-year-old Coronado, whose leadership qualities he trusted.

Coronado's army was one of the finest organized by the Spanish for the purpose of conquest. A total of 336 soldiers had assembled in the town of Compostela, 500 miles northwest of Mexico City, and on February 22, 1540, the viceroy himself sent them forth. Viceroy Mendoza had more than an official interest in this expedition; he and his friends (including Coronado himself) had vast sums invested in the project, which required roughly the equivalent of $3 million to finance.

The expeditionary force included a multinational contingent of five Portuguese, two Italians, a Frenchman, a Scot, a German, and three women in addition to a small group of friars (including Marcos de Niza). Several hundred Indian servants, over a thousand head of horses, and a great herd of cattle, sheep, and goats trailed behind.

The slow journey northward tried the patience of the restless soldiers, and the barren landscapes of the *despoblado* (uninhabited region) between the Gila River and the Zuñi pueblos only fanned their frustration. As the vast herds dwindled, hunger cast an ugly mood on the army, and Fray Marcos had to endure the scorn of his compatriots.

Finally, as the summer sun brightened the turquoise sky of the Zuñi lands, the army of metal-clad men on strange beasts approached from the south. A pilgrimage of Zuñi priests visiting a sacred shrine downstream along the Zuñi River had seen the invaders. By the time Coronado approached the Zuñi pueblos a few days later, they had been evacuated of women and children, and young warriors were poised

to defend their domain.

The sight of mud villages "crumpled together" quickly vanquished the Spaniards' golden fantasy. Their hunger now was merely for food; they were starving. Sacred Zuñi cornmeal on the ground surrounding the pueblo of Hawikuh would not deter the Europeans. The Battle of Hawikuh was engaged, a fateful clash of prayers, greed, stones, crossbows, arrows, and armor.

For an hour the Zuñis fought off the Europeans, even knocking Coronado off his horse with a shower of rocks. But after a dozen Zuñi warriors had been killed in battle, they retreated, abandoning the pueblo for the Spaniards to plunder. The Spaniards looted the maize

*31.* INTERIOR OF ZUÑI PUEBLO, *photograph, by Ben Wittick. The interior living quarters of Zuñi Pueblo, shown here about 1890, were sparse but practical. (Museum of New Mexico, Santa Fe, Neg. 58849)*

*32.* ZUÑI JAR, *photograph, by Kenneth Chapman. (Museum of New Mexico Photo Archives, Santa Fe, Neg. No. 22875)*

*33. (Opposite page)* ZUÑI MAIDEN, *photograph, by Edward S. Curtis. Pioneer photographer Edward S. Curtis captured a youthful optimism in this young Zuñi maiden's face nearly a century ago. (Museum of New Mexico, Santa Fe, 144510)*

stored in the pueblo but found no gold or silver.

Thus began the Spanish conquest and colonization of what would become known as Nuevo México, the "new" Mexico. Between 1540 and 1542, Coronado's explorations throughout the wonderful new land along the Rio Grande, the Great River of the North, extended across six states and encompassed an area equivalent to that of Western Europe.

Coronado's lieutenants explored a tremendous expanse of what we now call the Southwest. Pedro de Tovar and his small scouting party discovered the Hopi empire of villages in northern Arizona called Tusayan. García López de Cárdenas was the first European to gaze upon the Grand Canyon of the Colorado River. Melchior Díaz ventured into what we call California, named for Queen Califia, who ruled the fabled lands of the Amazon women. Hernando de Alvarado was the first to explore the city-states of Ácoma, Tiguex, Taos, and Pecos and the buffalo plains on the eastern horizon.

But Coronado was to be tricked again. On his eastern reconnaissance, Alvarado had encountered an Indian, called the "Turk" by the Spaniards because he looked like one, who described a fabulous province called Quivira. Quivira glistened far in the east, beyond the buffalo. Gold, silver, jewels, and silks were among the riches to be found in the great cities of the province. Quivira was ruled by King Tattarax, who slept in the afternoon under a large tree whose branches bowed with the weight of golden bells. As the wind swayed, the tree's boughs tinkled soft music that lulled the king to sleep.

The Turk claimed that Bigotes, so-called for his moustache, a loyal and friendly Pecos chief, possessed a golden bracelet from Quivira. Bigotes, unable to produce the mythical bracelet, was cruelly imprisoned by the Spaniards whose greed blinded their reason.

Actually a place called Quivira did exist. Ap-

parently, *Quivira* was a Pecos word for the homeland of the Wichita people of Kansas. Recent archaeological digs have even uncovered Pueblo pottery fragments that indicate some trading took place between the Plains Indians of Kansas and the southwestern tribes. As Coronado's army traveled eastward in the spring of 1541, the Teya Indians of the Texas panhandle described Quivira's inhabitants as very poor people who lived in grass huts.

Dispatching all except thirty soldiers back to New Mexico, Coronado ventured northward into Kansas, determined to satisfy his curiosity. Incredibly, the Spaniards encountered a blind Indian man who remembered a strange group of white men and a black man who were miraculous healers wandering the country farther south many, many days ago.

Coronado's group reached a spot close to Abilene, Kansas, before he gave up the golden fantasy. He found no Seven Cities and no Quivira. Many of his men remained, convinced that riches awaited them *más allá*, further on. But the great expedition was a failure, and

*34. Buffalo Dance, Zuñi, lithograph. This late nineteenth-century print depicts the Zuñi Buffalo Dance, still celebrated today. At left is the mission of Nuestra Señora de Guadalupe, built in the seventeenth century and restored in the late 1960s. (Collection of the author)*

Coronado's army retreated to Mexico in the spring of 1542.

Don Francisco Vásquez de Coronado returned a wiser man but surely brokenhearted. He had served his king and viceroy well, losing only ten men during the entire expedition. Viceroy Mendoza did not reprimand Coronado, who retained his post as governor of Nueva Galicia, ultimately rising to the position of *procurador* of Mexico City in 1551. When he died in 1554, the great myth of the Seven Cities of Cíbola died with him.

Yet because of his persistence in following his dream, Coronado's story continues to enthrall. His name is immortalized in the golden city of Santa Fe, where it appears as the name of a shopping center, a retail store, and merchandise of all types.

Cíbola and Quivira have become synonymous with Oz, places where all dreams come true and golden cities exist. And while finding these places may be impossible, the search is its own reward, as Coronado's legacy proves.

## Colonization of New Mexico

The failure of Coronado's quixotic adventure quelled Spanish interest in New Mexico for forty years. In the 1580s and 1590s, a series of exploratory *entradas* (entrances) were unsuccessful in identifying any worthwhile resources to exploit—other than human. Only the Church would be served by the colonization of the desolate northern province of New Mexico.

But Coronado's dream had not completely vanished. Perhaps Quivira really did exist. What lay beyond the known territory? If nothing else, a royal colony in New Mexico would provide a base of operations for new adventures of discovery. The viceroy was besieged by would-be colonizers who properly filled out the ponderous paperwork and applications for King Phillip II of Spain to approve. But not until 1598 did the creaking machinery of Spanish bureaucracy

finally grant Juan de Oñate the titles of governor, captain-general, and *adelantado*.

Oñate was said to be one of the five wealthiest men in Mexico, even as rumors of his financial squandering swirled about. His wife claimed descent from the Aztec emperor Montezuma and also Cortés himself. The Oñates seemed destined for greatness. Across the Atlantic, King Phillip II lay dying in his palace, the Escorial. About the time he died, in September 1598, a new Spanish colony was born along the banks of the Rio Grande.

For ten years the colonists struggled to survive at the "capital" city of San Gabriel, founded near an abandoned pueblo at the junction of the Chama River and the Rio Grande, near Española, about thirty miles north of Santa Fe. The original group of settlers, numbering 129 men, was reinforced in 1600 by 67 soldiers, 24 women and children, and 21 Indian servants. Harvests were unpredictable, and the colonists endured by "appropriating" food from the Pueblo Indians. Working the land was difficult, and many deserted San Gabriel. Complaints of Oñate's ineffectiveness began to reach

*35.* SPANISH PIONEER WOMAN, *drawing, by José Cisneros. In 1600, twenty-four women and sixty-seven soldiers reinforced the original 1598 New Mexican colonial expedition of Juan de Oñate. (Courtesy University of Texas at El Paso Press)*

the viceroy. In turn, Oñate complained of lack of support for the colony from Mexico. In 1607, the first governor of New Mexico resigned.

New Mexico might have been abandoned once again at this time, but Fray Lázaro Ximénez reported to his superiors the conversion of 7,000 native souls to Christianity in 1608. That year Pedro de Peralta was named to replace Oñate as governor of New Mexico and instructed to found a new villa so that the colonists could begin to live "with some order and decency." Peralta founded the new capital in 1609 and called it the City of Holy Faith, or Santa Fe.

## A Twentieth-Century Spanish Fantasy

Growing up in New Mexico or living in the Southwest for a length of time, one inevitably ponders the facts, myths, and legacy of the Spanish colonization. Certainly the myriad manifestations of the Spanish influence have been the subject of much scholarly and popular scrutiny.

The blood of the original colonists still flows within the veins of many New Mexicans. Only in New Mexico today are the terms Hispanic and Hispanic-American perfectly appropriate,

36. Taos Pueblo. Spanish explorer Hernando de Alvarado and his men first reached Taos Pueblo in October 1540, where they found the inhabitants clothed in apparel made of deerskin and buffalo hides. (Photograph by the author)

whereas in other parts of the United States, other descriptive terms such as Latino or Chicano are considered more "politically correct."

The fact is that for many New Mexicans of Hispanic descent, and also for other peoples still affected by the original *entradas* in 1539 and 1540, Spain herself remains an enigma. The Spain of the seventeenth and eighteenth centuries seems more familiar than the triumphant modern Castile of 1992.

Hispanic New Mexicans are haunted by images of the armed, intrepid conquistador on horseback; the lonely and utterly vulnerable

*hacienda* on the mountain frontier; or the brooding *padre* within his adobe sanctuary contemplating the impenetrable ceremonies of the Pueblo people. Of these images and others, a romantic quilt of old Nuevo México has been crafted, a fantasy itself, and a silent prayer for the mother country—Spain.

It is a secret, perhaps subconscious longing. Many New Mexicans of Spanish ancestry yearn to complete the circle and return in some way or other to Spain. Images of Spain beckon—guitars playing melancholy strains, majestic white and chestnut horses of Andalusia, ancient

*37. Toledo, Spain. Toledo, located fifty kilometers south of Madrid, dominated the royal, intellectual, and cultural life of the kingdom of Castille for centuries during the Middle Ages. From here, the brooding art of El Greco and the fantasy of Don Quixote helped shape Spanish character. (Photograph by the author)*

Spanish galleons crossing the Atlantic.

But the roots of what we think of as Spanish style extend into North Africa as well. The arches, domes, and enclosed courtyard gardens of North African architecture echo the influence of the Islamic rulers of Spain. Traces of Jewish design motifs blend seamlessly with Islamic and European elements to produce the architecture that is classically "Spanish." When this polygenetic architecture was combined with the adobe used by the Pueblo Indians, it produced the distinctive look of the romantic Southwest.

The legacy of Spain in New Mexico is a long and fascinating story, the topic of countless books and articles published over the years.

New Mexico still embraces its European and North African roots, which constitute a significant part of its charm.

The spirit of Spain still breathes deeply in the land, the laws, the villages, the rivers and *acequias* (irrigation ditches), the music, and the language. Yet part of Spain has been lost in New Mexico, forgotten and worn away by time. Some of the oppression and arrogance and xenophobia of the Spanish empire has faded away, and perhaps the best of Aragon and Castile remains in Santa Fe. Undoubtedly King Phillip II in 1598 would never have dreamed that this humble and forgotten outpost beneath the Sangre de Cristo Mountains could one day rise so high in the world's estimation.

38. *Moroccan village. The mud architecture of Morocco surely influenced Spanish builders in New Mexico, where they found similar climatic conditions. The rural architecture of Morocco still bears striking similarities to its southwestern counterpart. (Photograph by the author)*

39. *(Opposite page) The Alhambra, Granada, Spain. Today, many New Mexicans are discovering long-forgotten cultural links to Moorish and Sephardic Jewish traditions. In the province of Andalucía, the Alhambra of Granada stands as a symbol of the polyglot heritage of Spain. (Photograph by the author)*

# TRADE IN THE HIGH DESERT

or nearly two centuries, Santa Fe has reigned as a preeminent and exotic trading mecca, a place where calico and Mexican serapes were exchanged, where Spanish pieces of eight and American dollars could lure adventurous souls to new destinies and new horizons.

Although Santa Fe is still somewhat isolated (it has no major airline service), the people of New Mexico have produced arts and crafts, including textiles, pottery, jewelry, and food, of such high quality that they have been eagerly courted by merchants for centuries. Today, New Mexican products are known throughout the world and within the past few years have inspired a major design boom that has captivated the attention of the American public and also major fashion talents.

Considered a poor territory for most of its history by Spanish and American authorities, New Mexico has preserved a motherlode of wealth in its material culture. Worldwide appreciation of its unusual products has finally emerged in the twentieth century.

About eight hundred years ago, the indigenous peoples had already begun to trade with other native peoples in the Southwest and Mexico. Pottery made by the Ancient Ones and by the Pueblo Indians has been the area's most stable and consistent trade product, and in the ancient Southwest it was bartered for meat, wild cotton, hides, and other foodstuffs.

The discovery of fourteen macaw skeletons in one room at Chaco Canyon several decades ago, along with copper bells and sea shells found at other ruins, finally proved that extensive trade existed among the prehistoric peoples of the Southwest and Mexico.

Incredibly straight ancient roads emanate from Chaco Canyon, which indicate the existence of a remarkable network of communication and trade routes between native communities of the classic period (approximately A.D. 1000–1300). Pottery along with woven goods such as clothing, sandals, and jewelry provided a stable economy and a comfortable lifestyle for the Ancient Ones, helping them to achieve their wondrous feats of architecture.

With the arrival of the Spanish, Pueblo trade

40. (Opposite page) Salt train, unloaded, Sandoval Street, Santa Fe, June 1880. Even though the Atchison, Topeka and Santa Fe Railroad had entered New Mexico Territory a year before the date of this photograph, sturdy Mexican jack mules still carried essential commodities across the frontier. The popularity of the territorial style of architecture, a marriage of indigenous adobe building and Greek revival styling introduced by the U.S. Army, is clearly evident in this historic view of Santa Fe's commercial district. (Photograph by Ben Wittick; courtesy of School of American Research Collections in the Museum of New Mexico, Neg. No. 15815)

with Mexico and other Native Americans was radically transformed. The province had little to offer the viceroy in Mexico City. About the only New Mexican products the Spanish thought worth returning to Spain were buffalo and other animal hides. Meanwhile, during the seventeenth century and especially the eighteenth century, Spanish and Mexican products and technologies were transported to the remote northern province.

Spanish colonial arts and crafts fashioned in New Mexico are unique, possessing a rustic, primitive quality. Lack of tools, materials, pig-

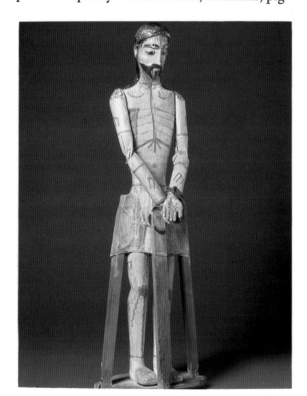

ments, and aesthetic standards fostered an inventive "naive" style that has survived and continues to be a major element of the Santa Fe trading bonanza.

Spanish friars and colonists trained apprentices (including many Pueblo Indians) as carpenters to produce architectural woodwork and furniture. Based on medieval and Renaissance prototypes, New Mexican furniture was laboriously produced by hand, chip-carved, and fastened together by mortise-and-tenon joinery. It appeared crude and ill-proportioned. But these very qualities have been preserved, emulated, and now idealized as New Mexican colonial furniture has been embraced as a classic American style.

In other crafts, such as the making of relig-

ious *santos* (carvings representing images of the saints), *bultos* (sculptures in the round of saints and other sacred personages), *retablos* (flat, painted wall plaques of saints and holy figures), and tinwork, the Spanish colonial aesthetic is distinctive. Dolorous expressions painted in organic pigments, often boldly displaying the bloody wounds of martyrdom, produce a haunting, mystical effect. New Mexican religious folk art is also fanatically collected.

## Spanish Colonial Trading

Despite its ponderous bureaucratic trading policies, the Spanish administration in Santa Fe

41. *(Upper left) Anasazi trade goods. Pre-Columbian Pueblo traders bartered pottery and woven goods for food, meat, and hides from neighboring tribes. (Photograph by Bill Keeler)*

42. *(Lower left)* OUR FATHER OF NAZARETH, *bulto by José Benito Ortega (1858–1941). Among the most prolific of New Mexican santeros, José Benito Ortega created at least 200 bultos such as this one while working as a traveling carver in northeastern New Mexico. Ortega is the creator of the so-called "Mora style," recognized by the flat dimensional modeling and the downcast expression. (National Museum of American Art, Washington, D.C.)*

43. *Detail of a buckskin dress with beaded decorations, Plains culture, circa 1900. Buffalo hides and tanned animal hides crafted by the Plains nomadic tribes (primarily the Kiowas and Comanches) were highly prized from the late eighteenth century throughout the nineteenth century. This classic look of tanned leather and beadwork thrives today in Santa Fe's finest boutiques. (Panhandle-Plains Museum, Canyon, Texas)*

helped establish the trade fairs, held on a sporadic but almost annual basis (depending on the status of ongoing hostilities), at the Taos and Pecos pueblos. Taos, spectacularly seated in the mountains on the northern edge of the colonial settlement, attracted Utes, Kiowas, Comanches, and other Rocky Mountain and Plains tribes to

barter. Pecos Pueblo, located twenty miles east of Santa Fe at the mouth of a gaping canyon, beckoned the buffalo traders.

Primarily a phenomenon after 1750, the trade fairs were eagerly anticipated by all parties and lasted several days, often amidst the brilliant colors of October aspens, oaks, and cottonwoods. These gala affairs were among the first "powwows" or "gatherings of nations" staged in the Old West.

From the Great Plains on New Mexico's eastern flank, the Comanches and Apaches brought buffalo meat and tanned buffalo hides and robes. The Utes from the north brought tanned elk, deer, and antelope hides, which were especially sought after. The leather goods traded by the nomadic Indians were one of the

few New Mexican exports shipped to Mexico and Spain and would have been a more valuable source of commerce for New Mexico had the mother country been subject to harder winters.

The Pueblo Indians traded pottery, corn, and baskets, while the Spanish provided woven "Rio Grande" blankets and metal tools. Horses and captured Indian slaves—often young girls

44. (Left) Leather shield with birds, Kiowa, circa 1890. Native objects of great importance, such as this Kiowa war shield, could express sublime qualities of art and craftsmanship. (Panhandle-Plains Museum, Canyon, Texas)

45. (Upper right) Spanish colonial chest. Sturdy, chip-carved storage chests were prized possessions in New Mexican households during the colonial period. This chest displays Moorish-influenced carving and designs which continue to influence contemporary Santa Fe furniture designers. (Museum of New Mexico, Santa Fe)

46. (Lower right) NUESTRA SEÑORA DE GUADALUPE, retablo, by Pedro Antonio Fresquís (died 1831). One of the earliest true santeros in the New Mexican tradition is Pedro Antonio Fresquís, who created interesting effects in his retablos by incising lines into the paint to reveal color underneath. (National Museum of American Art, Washington, D. C.)

captured from various tribes by marauding Apaches and Comanches—were treasured by Spanish households and were often given by a man to his new bride as a wedding gift.

The trade fairs were unpredictable and dramatic, as warring tribes occasionally showed up at the same time. Plains Indians exacted instant retribution, at knife- or spearpoint, if they felt cheated by a dealer. Villages could still be raided at the close of a fair, even though an informal truce existed. But the trade fairs introduced the exchange of European and Native American products that is at the heart of the Santa Fe trading fantasy and remains one of the adobe capital's main attractions.

While Spain effectively controlled her international trade, isolating Santa Fe from French and American merchants, her own traders ventured far north and west. Spanish goods reached as far north as British Columbia and Idaho, and Santa Fe goods were known in North Dakota by 1790.

## The Comanchero Trade

In the eighteenth century, after de Vargas's reconquest following the Pueblo Revolt of 1680, the Comanchero trade (based on the hunting of buffalo) emerged as a major source of economic activity in New Mexico. Spanish,

47. *Pottery vendors, San Juan Pueblo, 1935. After World War I, New Mexico's growing tourism industry enabled the growth of cottage arts and crafts industries such as the sale of pottery in the Pueblo communities, as depicted here at San Juan Pueblo, near Española. (Photograph by T. Harmon Parkhurst, Museum of New Mexico Photo Archives, Santa Fe, Neg. No. 22671)*

Mexican, and Pueblo traders from the Rio Grande Valley traveled east across the Llano Estacado (staked plains) and met nomadic southern Plains tribes at several selected campsites in West Texas and the Texas panhandle. Tecovas Springs near Amarillo, Yellow Houses near Lubbock, Las Lenguas (the tongues) near Quitaque, and Palo Duro (hard stick) near Canyon all hosted lively bartering sessions.

In the early 1800s, Spanish traders expanded the Plains trade to include visits to the Kiowas along the Arkansas River, the Arapahos in eastern Colorado, and even the Pawnees, who roamed the riverbanks of the Platte River in Nebraska.

The New Mexican traders enticed Comanches and Kiowas with horses, saddles, bits and bridles, woven blankets, iron weapons and tools, and metal jewelry. The Plains Indians in return offered buffalo robes, deerskins, buckskin clothing, and dried meat as barter.

When the haggling got intense, New Mexican merchants sweetened the deal by offering Mexican tobacco known as *punche* and other delicacies such as brown sugar, beans, piñon nuts, corn, and chile peppers. The Plains Indians also had a weakness for turquoise and abalone shells.

The Comanchero trade in New Mexico re-

flects another romantic aspect of a fascinating trading tradition. The routes into the southern Plains were well trafficked throughout most of the nineteenth century. By 1880, the railroads, the Indian wars, and the wanton slaughter of millions of buffalo finally spelled doom for the Comanchero trade.

Entire villages, especially at the eastern fringes near Pecos Pueblo, thrived on the Comanchero trade, observing with rituals and

ceremonies the departure and arrival of the caravans. Along the banks of the Pecos River, San José, San Miguel, and Villanueva grew rapidly after 1821, when Mexico won her independence. And Las Vegas farther east became a prime center for both the Comancheros and the Santa Fe Trail merchants.

## New Opportunities and Trade Routes

Long before Spain lost her colonial empire in the north, other nations had sought opportunities to break through Spanish restrictions and extend trade through her territory. The mirage of the golden city had been tantalizing French trappers from the time they reached the lower Mississippi River in 1720. Brothers Pierre and Paul Mallet succeeded in reaching Taos and Santa Fe in 1739, and between 1749 and 1752 at least four other parties of Frenchmen had found Santa Fe. Nine French-made hats and nine pairs of shoes made of beaver skin were confiscated by Spanish officials in 1752.

France lost the Louisiana Territory to Spain in 1763, and for forty more years (until the Louisiana Purchase by the United States in 1803), New Mexico remained hopelessly isolated. Once the awesome Louisiana Territory became American territory, the lure of the elusive northern outpost of the Spanish gleamed bright once again.

Despite their bold attempts, such adventurers as James Purcell and Manuel Lisa, a Spanish entrepreneur, were not able to provide access to the Rio Grande. Nevertheless, in what appears to be one of the West's earliest spy missions, Zebulon Pike and twenty-two companions succeeded in exploring the Plains country for the United States and getting arrested by Spanish authorities along the upper Rio Grande. During their subsequent transport to Santa Fe and Chihuahua, Pike carefully recorded his impressions, which were released in a report in 1810.

Pike described a land—New Mexico—begging for contact with the outside world, with plenty of hard currency to offer in exchange for luxury items such as cotton and silk fabric, shoes, and metal tools. It was a lure that few could resist.

Americans watched with increasing fascina-

*51. Martinez Hacienda, Taos. The early nineteenth-century Martinez Hacienda of Taos is perhaps the best-preserved example of a New Mexican fortified household. Wagons of the northern Taos branch of the Santa Fe Trail surely stopped here for rest, business, and entertainment. (Photo by the author)*

tion in the early nineteenth century as Mexico struggled to free herself from the heavy Spanish yoke. Fate was smiling sweetly on redheaded Captain William Becknell when he advertised in the June 25, 1821, edition of the *Missouri Intelligencer* for a "company of men destined to the westward for the purpose of trading for horses and mules, and catching wild animals of every description." About the same time that Becknell's expedition reached the Arkansas River, in September 1821, Mexico won her independence, and soon he was urged on by joyous Mexican troops who escorted his entourage through San Miguel del Vado and on to the forbidden city at last.

Becknell, making the most of his opportunity, had opened the trade route that came to be known as the Santa Fe Trail and thus connected the western U.S. frontier with rich markets to the west. On a cold January day in 1822, Becknell and his men arrived back home in Franklin, Missouri. As Becknell slashed open his leather saddlebags, stamped silver pesos cascaded onto the town's cobblestone streets, each coin reflecting a fantasy of a distant city in the eyes of the onlookers. Thus began the second trail across Kansas in pursuit of Quivira.

During the early years of the Santa Fe Trail, American fur and beaver trappers flocked to New Mexico, and canny merchants discovered that even greater profits could be realized by forging a new trade route from Santa Fe to Chihuahua. American goods quickly flooded the Santa Fe market, and the town's limited supply of coined money was exhausted. The emerging Chihuahua trade and the bartering of New Mexican beaver pelts, hides, and sturdy Mexican mules (which were sold in St. Louis for great profit) kept up the flow of Americans headed toward Santa Fe.

New Mexicans eagerly awaited the caravans, which were saluted in the small villages by clanging church bells and throngs of excited people hoping to hawk meat, cheese, and gar-

den vegetables for anything the Americans had to offer. Coveted items brought from Missouri included metal farm tools such as hoes, plows, and sickles; carpenter tools such as wood planes, saws, axes, hammers, nails, and screws; and building hardware such as padlocks and windowpanes. Glass did not immediately become a feature of New Mexican homes, however. The U.S. Army of Occupation in 1846 reported that only the Governor's Palace had glass windows, and it still had animal hides functioning as doors in some rooms. Women shopped for gaily colored cotton, calico, and imported European textiles; thimbles and needles; coffeepots; mirrors; combs; perfumes; bowls; and clocks. Cof-

52. *Wagon train, New Mexico, 1894. This drawing by Dan Suiter, titled* Perilous Wagoning in New Mexico Using the Dragbrake in Descending a Jump-off, *captures the spirit of danger and adventure of the Santa Fe Trail era. (Museum of New Mexico, Santa Fe, Neg. No. 109021)*

fee and liquor were other prized acquisitions.

In the quarter century following the blazing of the road to Santa Fe, an important trading detour south to Mexico was developed. During the colonial period, New Mexico was dependent on supply caravans that traveled the Camino Real (royal road). The Camino Real linked seven cities between Mexico City and Santa Fe. Thus New Mexico was totally dependent on its southern lifeline and was at the mercy of unscrupulous traders in Chihuahua. Santa Fe Trail traders soon gutted the New Mexican market and simply took the excess goods into Chihuahua, another 500 miles south. Within two decades, the value of the Chihuahua trade greatly eclipsed that of Santa Fe.

As Santa Fe served as a hub of burgeoning international trade, its residents had begun to enjoy a much higher standard of living. Economic interdependence was fostered between the American traders and the New Mexicans. As accounts, diaries, and journals of trail adventures filtered back east, a new romantic portrait of the southwestern frontier emerged. Dashing *vaqueros*, dark-eyed *señoritas*, Pueblos and Navajos wrapped in colorful blankets, and handsome

American traders and adventurers—these clichés were pure grist for popular dime novels about the West. They continue to have an enduring fascination and are still part of the repertoire of Hollywood and Madison Avenue.

### The Bloodless Conquest

Perhaps the most important consequence of the opening of the Santa Fe Trail was that it effectively prepared the populace and economy of Mexico's northern province for a bloodless American conquest. In response to hostilities between the United States and Mexico, Brigadier General Stephen Watts Kearney was ordered to assemble an army at Fort Leavenworth, Kansas, and to seize Santa Fe in 1846. Kearney did so on August 18, ending the brief period of Mexican rule. By 1848, the war with Mexico was over, and New Mexico formally became an American territory.

The Santa Fe Trail trade was hardly affected by the transition and grew heavier after the war. Indians on the eastern Great Plains continued to threaten the trade caravans, and in 1851 the army built Fort Union in northeastern New

*53. Mechanics corral, Fort Union, 1866. Established near the junction of the Mountain and Cimarron forks of the Santa Fe Trail, thirty miles northeast of Las Vegas, Fort Union provided refuge and also valuable maintenance and supply facilities. The busy mechanics corral, seen here, saw the repair of hundreds of wagons during the heyday of the Santa Fe Trail. (Photograph by the U.S. Army Signal Corps, Museum of New Mexico, Santa Fe, Neg. No. 1835)*

Mexico as a peacekeeping stronghold. A few years earlier, Fort Marcy was built in Santa Fe to house the army of occupation.

The increase in the American presence in New Mexico after the Mexican War brought with it an increase in commerce. The U.S. Army's efforts to protect the Santa Fe Trail and quell hostile Indian raiders created the need for more forts and soldiers in the New Mexico Territory. These in turn required great quantities of food, supplies, and livestock, which private businessmen gladly supplied.

After 1850, a new breed of Santa Fe trader emerged. Entrepreneurs such as the Bent brothers and Ceran St. Vrain exploited a vast empire from their base in Taos and at Bent's Fort on the Arkansas River. Hispanic Comancheros, veterans of the buffalo trade, also prospered. In Las Vegas, fortunes were realized, and grand mansions were built by the

Romero and Baca brothers, Francisco López, and Miguel A. Otero.

New opportunities in the Southwest also lured a resourceful group of Bavarian Jews to follow their dreams. In Santa Fe, the Speigelberg and Zeckendorf brothers became prominent businessmen, and Charles Ilfeld and Emmanuel Rosenwald built large trading companies on the Las Vegas Plaza. By 1900, Las Vegas, Santa Fe, and Albuquerque were home to significant Jewish communities.

Just as the Santa Fe Trail and the U.S. Army shook New Mexico out of its slumber, so, too, did the snorting black symbol of a new era—the locomotive—propel the land of the Ancient Ones forward as if by time machine. The awesome power of the railroad quickly transformed communities, businesses, and households in New Mexico and ushered in a new cosmopolitan lifestyle along the banks of the Rio Grande. Not

*54. Las Vegas Plaza, circa 1885. The Santa Fe Railroad's dramatic entry into New Mexico Territory in 1879 transformed Las Vegas (and Albuquerque) into thriving cities overnight. The architecture of Las Vegas Plaza already reflects prosperity in this 1885 view. (Photo by F. E. Evans, Museum of New Mexico, Neg. No. 50798)*

all towns and villages tasted the fruits of progress, however. Remote mountain villages still retained an almost medieval way of life while less than 100 miles away Victorian mansions were being built in Santa Fe and Las Vegas.

Although the railroad brought the Gilded Age to New Mexico, temporarily blinding New Mexicans to the glories of their own culture, Indian traders in the West were using the steel tracks to ship exotic Native American products to the eastern seaboard. Pioneer traders such as Lorenzo Hubbel of Ganado and C. N. Cotton of Gallup printed "catalogs" lauding the quality and beauty of Navajo rugs. Soon the freight cars of the Santa Fe Railroad carried Navajo rugs and Pueblo pottery and jewelry to such cities as New York, Philadelphia, and Chicago.

Thus, by the early twentieth century, all of the elements of a unique, fabulous, and completely southwestern trading mecca had been established. Prehistoric, Pueblo, Navajo, Apache, and Plains art and artifacts as well as the handicrafts of many other Native American tribes are now displayed alongside the many treasures of Mexico, Spain, Spanish colonial New Mexico, and South America. And recently the Santa Fe trading fantasy has been enhanced even more by cowboy culture, the availability of New Age talismans such as crystals and gems, and a score of intellectual gold mines such as rare books and ephemera. As always, the Indians sell their wares under the portal on the plaza in the middle of downtown Santa Fe.

Santa Fe remains today what it was two centuries ago, an adobe mecca where the wealth of many peoples glitters under the turquoise sky.

*55. Pueblo Indian vendors, Palace of the Governors, 1935. Pueblo Indian vendors began selling their attractive pottery and jewelry in public places such as Albuquerque's Alvarado Hotel and Santa Fe's Palace of the Governors after 1900. (Museum of New Mexico, Santa Fe, Neg. No. 6849)*

56. Indians continue to sell their wares at the Palace of the Governors in the 1990s. The long portal of Santa Fe's Palace of the Governors hosts a spectacular display of Native American craftspeople and fascinated shoppers every day. (Photograph by the author)

57. Indian Market, Santa Fe; a row of booths on the plaza. Santa Fe's annual Indian Market, held during the third week of August, attracts nearly 100,000 visitors. Hundreds of vendors' booths line the historic plaza and spill out onto side streets. St. Francis Cathedral is shown in the background. (Photograph by Murrae Haynes, 1993; courtesy Southwestern Association on Indian Affairs, Inc. [SWAIA], Santa Fe)

58. *Santa Fe collectibles. Among the many offerings available in Santa Fe stores and boutiques are Spanish colonial- and cowboy- style furniture; postmodern steel canopy beds by designer Lloyd Kreitz; an infinite variety of decorator accessories with a southwestern flavor; authentic buckskin and frontier clothing by designer Cathy Smith; Navajo "broomstick dresses" and other modern adaptations from Native American tradition, as well as Navajo rugs—the classic heirloom of the Southwest that is now collected throughout the world. (Photographs courtesy of Simply Santa Fe, located on the south side of the plaza)*

59. Santa Fe's international style. Santa Fe has welcomed an eclectic approach to fashion with a distinctive Third World appeal. In addition to regional classics such as the Navajo concho belt and southwestern turquoise and silver jewelry, exotic fabrics from Latin America and beads and jewelry from India, Morocco, Mexico, and Africa are increasingly part of the Santa Fe "look." Unique high-fashion outfits by internationally known designers are available in Santa Fe's favorite stores. (Photographs courtesy of Origins, located on San Francisco Street, Santa Fe).

# ARTISTS OF VISION

Santa Fe is currently the third largest art market in the United States, which seems appropriate for a region that has long produced some of North America's most spectacular art. The rich tradition of Native American artwork continues to grow and unfold, and now Western European art influences, melding with Native American inspirations, have led in the twentieth century to an art that is by turns romantic, spiritual, meditative, bold, and shocking in character.

Today Santa Fe art depicts images of sensuous, spectacular, yet melancholy landscapes. Canvases interpret religious ceremonies of the Pueblo, Navajo, and Hispanic Catholic traditions. Realistic western images continue their longtime popularity, while innovative expressions of southwestern popular culture in 1990 announced a "postmodernist" sensibility.

A casual visitor to a few Santa Fe art galleries is likely to encounter a great variety of art images ranging from the triteness of the omnipresent howling coyote and Kokopelli figures to the sophistication of sculptures fabricated from the wasted hi-tech nuclear equipment parts from nearby Los Alamos National Laboratory.

## Traditional Native Art

The southwestern United States has long been fertile soil for mystical artists—those who at-

60. (Opposite page) BLUE RIVER, oil on canvas, Georgia O'Keeffe. Georgia O'Keeffe's monumental paintings of the New Mexico landscape are enduring southwestern icons. (New Mexico Museum of Fine Arts, Santa Fe)

tempt to portray in their work the relationship between the visible world and the invisible world; and the relationship between humankind and the cosmos. Among the earliest recorded images in the region are thousands of petroglyphs etched on soft sandstone or volcanic rocks. Enigmatic drawings of origin myths, kachinas (spiritual beings), mythological creatures, and humans can be deciphered next to drawings of animals such as deer and snakes. Perhaps these petroglyphs record the legendary wanderings of the People and their clans as they made their way to the sacred homeland. Certainly some murals on forsaken canyon walls record early visions of the cosmos and all-powerful kachinas.

The original southwestern peoples developed settled cultures after A.D. 500. Subterranean kivas, or spiritual chambers, were built almost simultaneously with the first earthen and wooden shelters. The earliest native artists

learned where to find natural pigments for paints and applied the subtle earth colors to interior kiva walls. The kiva art of the Ancient Ones is among the most celebrated of all southwestern art, depicting zoomorphic kachinas that combine the body parts of humans with the limbs and heads of various other creatures, not unlike the griffins or centaurs of Greek mythology.

Clay became a highly developed and expressive material in the ancient southwestern native potter's hands. Pottery making was vigorously pursued by many of the ancient peoples, but it was especially important as a form of cultural expression for the Mimbres people, who inhabited the valleys of the Gila and Mimbres rivers of southwestern New Mexico (near Silver City) from about A.D. 1000–1400. The elegant black-and-white paintings on Mimbres pots are at times spiritual revelations and at other times clever depictions of everyday scenes such as trapping quail or harvesting corn. To connoisseurs today, Mimbres pottery is high art, dazzling in its graphic power and wit.

The powerful religious cosmology and traditions of the ancient native people and their descendants, the modern Pueblo Indians, have

produced other art forms with mystical and esoteric qualities. Carved stone and wooden sculptures of kachinas, power animals, and war gods have been fashioned over the centuries and usually housed in sacred kivas and shrines. Kachina doll carvings evolved as tools for teaching children about the gods. The Zuñis have excelled at the art of carving fetishes of various animals, miniature artworks crafted of stone or wood, usually of valued materials such as turquoise and accented with "prayer bundles" of feathers and other meaningful objects. The fetishes are talismans intended to bring good fortune and power to the owner.

Until the twentieth century, kiva art, pottery design, fetishes, kachina carvings, and ceremonial paintings on headdresses or other apparel were the major forms of symbolic and figurative

expression for the Pueblo Indians. Spiritual and visionary iconography, especially of the sacred pantheon of the kachinas, developed gradually over a period of about one thousand years and continues to have a profound influence on many Native American and Anglo artists.

*61. Mimbres culture bowl. Stylized figurative scenes of the everyday life of the Mimbres culture of southwestern New Mexico continue to be a major source of design inspiration for modern Pueblo and other southwestern artists. (Courtesy Gallery 10, Santa Fe)*

*62. Polychrome olla, signed Maria © 1934, by Maria and Julian Martinez, San Ildefonso Pueblo. (Photograph by Eric Swanson; courtesy Dewey Galleries, Ltd., Santa Fe)*

## The Spanish Influence

With the arrival of the Spanish colonists in New Mexico in the early seventeenth century, Roman Catholic religious art was introduced into the New Mexico colony and ultimately into the greater Southwest. Before its arrival in New Mexico, Spanish religious art had acquired a particularly devout, dolorous, and even surreal character.

The Spanish Crown during the golden age of 1492–1588 had the financial and political means to acquire the riches of European art now housed at the Prado Museum in Madrid. Masterpieces by Titian, Rubens, Brueghel, and Bosch were imported to Spain, influencing the aesthetic taste of the Crown, the aristocracy, the clergy, and the artists of the empire. Spanish masters such as El Greco, Zurbarán, and Goya refined the Spanish aesthetic of somber, brooding devotion embellished by slightly surreal distortion of human form and emotion. These qualities would take root in the distant New Mexico colony during the seventeenth and eighteenth centuries and influence all subsequent masters of Hispanic art in the Southwest.

With few available metal tools and no heavy machinery, Spanish Franciscan missionaries taught the Pueblo peoples refined skills in architecture, carpentry, and blacksmithing. Some religious art was imported from Mexico for the adobe sanctuaries, but the majority of sculptures (*bultos*) and wall plaques (*retablos*) were handcrafted by a few artists, who often traveled from village to village offering their services.

Early New Mexican Hispanic *santeros*, or carvers of saints—including Molleno and Pedro Antonio Fresquís and anonymous artists such as the Arroyo Hondo Santero—paved the way for a flowering of New Mexican religious art during the nineteenth century. As the New Mexico colony expanded into ever-more remote mountain valleys, the Catholic clergy were hard-pressed to serve all communities.

New Mexico developed a Catholic devo-

63. SAINT ANDREW AND SAINT FRANCIS, oil, by El Greco (1541–1614). El Greco resided most of his life in Toledo, the artistic, religious, and intellectual capital of sixteenth-century Spain. His slightly distorted perspective, elongated figures, and the emotional power of his restricted palette give his paintings transcendent emotional power. (Prado Museum, Madrid)

64. THE TRIUMPH OF DEATH, oil (detail), by Pieter Brueghel the Elder (died 1569). Pieter Brueghel's harrowing view of the apocalypse—skeletons reaping the bodies and souls of the living—was one of the Spanish Crown's prized possessions before becoming a crown jewel of the Prado Museum's collection. This imagery still survives in New Mexican Hispanic folk art in the popular death carts of La Muerte. (Prado Museum, Madrid)

65. TEMPTATION OF SAINT ANTHONY, oil, by Hieronymous Bosch (1450–1516). Widely acclaimed as the first surrealist works, the bizarre visions of Flemish master Hieronymous Bosch have haunted the European psyche for centuries. The theme of the temptation of Saint Anthony has remained popular in New Mexico folk art. (Prado Museum, Madrid)

tional fraternity called *La Hermandad de Nuestro Padre Jesús Nazareno* (Brotherhood of Our Father Jesus the Nazarene), more familiarly known as *Los Penitentes* (the Penitentes). The Brotherhood flourished in northern New Mexico and southern Colorado in the nineteenth century and early twentieth century, and devoted amateur artists of the Brotherhood produced much of the deeply moving, yet primitive religious art that continues to attract many admirers and collectors to Santa Fe.

Because of the overarching importance of Holy Week observances, much religious art of the Penitente *santeros* is devoted to saints and scenes related to the Passion, Crucifixion, and Resurrection of Christ. These popular themes include Christ Crucified, Our Lady of Sorrows, Jesus the Nazarene, Our Lady of Solitude, Christ in the Holy Sepulcher, Saint Joseph, and death carts carrying ghastly sculptures of *La Muerte* (Death).

Community and traveling *santeros* also fashioned images of patron saints for a community's chapel or a family. In New Mexico, Our Lady of Guadalupe, Saint Isidore the Farmer (patron of farmers), the Holy Child of Atocha, Saint Anthony of Padua, Saint Joseph the Patriarch, Saint Michael the Archangel, and Saint Francis of Assisi are favorites. Biblical scenes such as Saint Michael slaying the devil or the Holy Family's flight from Egypt are other subjects depicted in *retablos*.

*Santero* art in New Mexico evolved from crude depictions of religious themes on hides in the eighteenth century. Friars such as Fray Andrés García decorated many church interiors, and educated Spaniards such as mapmaker Don Bernardo Miera y Pacheco also fashioned religious images for the churches.

The early nineteenth century brought the recognition of the first clearly identifiable "artists," notably the Laguna Santero, Pedro Fresquís, and Molleno (also known as the "Chili" Painter for his distinctive red decorative flourishes).

66. SAN ISIDRO, *natural pigments on carved wood, by the Arroyo Hondo Santero (1830–1860). Saint Isidore the Farmer was so devoted to prayer and spiritual aspiration that angels were said to have helped plow his fields. The patron saint of farmers and agriculture, San Isidro is a favorite subject of New Mexican* santero *art. Fine detailing and sharp facial features distinguish the work of the anonymous Arroyo Hondo Santero. (Taylor Museum, Colorado Springs)*

67. VIRGIN MARY AND CHRIST CHILD, *paint on carved wood, by José Benito Ortega (1858–1941). Somewhat reminiscent of El Greco's elongated figure style, this quality of Ortega's work probably owes more to his use of conventional milled lumber for his* bultos. *Ortega was one of the most prolific of New Mexico* santeros *but stopped carving after 1907. (National Museum of American Art, Washington, D.C.)*

The middle decades of the nineteenth century fostered the refinement of *santero* art and is considered the classical period. Skilled painters such as José Aragón, José Rafael Aragón, the Santo Niño Santero, and the Quill Pen Santero were active from 1830–1860.

With the establishment of the Santa Fe Trail in 1821 and later the arrival of Archbishop Lamy of France in 1851, mass-market religious statues manufactured in Europe and East Coast cities and painted religious images began to displace handcrafted art. *Retablo* art began to decline; but in more isolated locations, the crafting of *bultos* reached new levels of artistic excellence. José Benito Ortega of Mora is the most recognizable master, and other well-known artists include José de García Gonzales, Juan Miguel Herrera, and Juan Ramón Velasáquez. Rich traditions of folk art also developed in Abiquiú and Taos after 1850.

The village of Córdova, just north of Chimayó, has provided an unbroken tradition of exceptional *santero* art which provides a transition from the work of José Rafael Aragón to the present. Another resident of Córdova, Nasario López, also made religious figures in the mid-nineteenth century. Related by marriage, the Aragón and López families produced exceptional artists through several generations, and influenced the development of *santero* art in the twentieth century.

After World War I, José Dolores López (1868–1937) began carving household objects with a distinctive new style, featuring delicate, filigree carving effects, whimsical themes, and charming compositions. His art was eagerly encouraged and collected by Santa Fe buyers. Many of his images were unpainted and naturally finished.

López's son George (1900–1993) carried on his father's style, and other carvers in Córdova have perfected the distinctive natural wood style. In Taos, Patrocinio Barela (1900–1964) evolved a similar technique infused with raw

68. VIRGIN AND CHILD, *natural pigments on carved wood, by José Rafael Aragón. Aragón's is often described as the most "classical" of New Mexican* santero *art. His technique of combining clear, well-defined draughtmanship and vibrant color continues to influence contemporary* santeros, *notably Ramón José López. (Museum of New Mexico, Santa Fe)*

69. DAVID AND GOLIATH, *wood, by Patrocinio Barela (1908–1964). Under the patronage of the Federal Art Project of the WPA, Taos woodcarver Patrocinio Barela evolved a highly individual, abstract, and modern style full of allegorical references and symbols. His powerful sculptures appealed to modern collectors, and Barela achieved a national reputation for his art, which was exhibited in major museums during his lifetime. (National Museum of American Art, Washington, D.C.)*

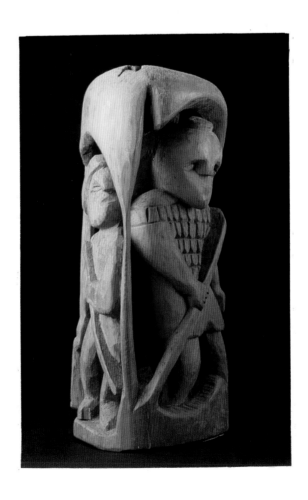

sculptural and inspired imagery.

The dramatic revival of contemporary *santero* art in the 1980s has produced several accomplished masters, enough to rival any period in history. The list is long and growing, but perhaps most notable is the rise of female artists such as Anita Romero Jones and Marie Romero Cash. The late Horacio Valdéz of Taos made exceptional images, and currently the field boasts young masters such as Luis Tapia, Felix López, Charles Carrillo, Ramón José López, Victor Goler, and Luisito Lujan. The *santero* art of New Mexico promises to blossom well into the twenty-first century.

## Influences of the Modern European Tradition

At the end of the nineteenth century New Mexico was culturally isolated, and traditional Native American and Hispanic artistic expressions remained relatively pure. At the turn of the century, many professional artists still flocked to Europe for artistic enlightenment, but a few, through accident or drawn by word of mouth, were beginning to venture to Santa Fe and Taos. Since that time, New Mexico's powerful attraction for artists of all persuasions has gained momentum with each passing decade.

By now, Santa Fe has been well known as an art mecca for nearly one hundred years, during which time its role in the art world has been to serve as a haven for creative spirits working outside the prevailing norms of the New York and Chicago art schools. Major international art movements such as impressionism, expressionism, and modernism found their way slowly to New Mexico, where they were modified by the landscape and culture and by the work of extraordinary talents such as John Marin, Andrew Dasburg, and Georgia O'Keeffe.

Still, as this century approaches its end, dominant artistic sensibilities established by pioneering artists of the Santa Fe and Taos schools provide a framework within which many of today's leading artists continue to work.

Great French painters of the impressionist era, such as Edgar Degas, Henri Toulouse-Lautrec, Claude Monet, and Georges Seurat, pioneered the representation of nature as the eye sees it. New theories of color helped the impressionist artists create light-filled paintings. Their approach to painting would heavily influence the Taos artists.

After the tremendous achievements of the impressionist school, a few European artists adapted the suddenly unrestricted paint palette to their own highly personal styles. Vincent Van Gogh and Paul Gauguin infused their vibrant paintings with highly charged emotional content. Paul Cézanne used an analytical approach that revealed the interrelationship of form and color. These great postimpressionists still influence some Santa Fe masters.

Elsewhere in the world, expressionism followed postimpressionism as a major movement in modern art. Just after the turn of the century, artists such as Henri Matisse, André Derain, Emil Nolde, and others pushed painting toward emotional and psychological expression rather than the pure perception of nature championed by the impressionists. Design was distorted to emphasize certain elements of a picture's composition (for example, enlarging a person's face or filling the canvas frame with a brooding sky). Expressionism has also found a niche in Santa Fe and is used to great effect particularly by Native American masters.

At roughly the same time, about 1910, Pablo Picasso and Georges Braque were inspired by African art and the work of Paul Cézanne to begin a unique artistic collaboration known as cubism. Their fascination with "primitive" art inspired others to search for inspiration in the art of the world's indigenous cultures. Primitivism was an important early modernist theme. Soon East Coast intellectuals would discover that New Mexico harbored a surviving "primi-

70. *(Opposite page)* INDIAN HUNTER, *oil on canvas, by Joseph H. Sharp (1859–1953). Joseph H. Sharp was determined to capture the romantic vanishing culture of the Indians on canvas, much as Edward S. Curtis was documenting them in photography. Sharp was most familiar with the Plains Indian cultures and often depicted Pueblo Indians dressed in Plains apparel. (Courtesy Zaplin-Lampert Gallery, Santa Fe)*

71. *(Opposite page)* THE YOUNG HUNTER, *oil on canvas, by E. I. Couse (1866–1936). Eanger Irving Couse enjoyed a profitable relationship with the Atchison, Topeka and Santa Fe Railroad, producing twenty-three images for their famous calendars between 1923 and 1936. This painting of a squatting, meditative Indian is typical of Couse's commercial style. (Courtesy Zaplin-Lampert Gallery, Santa Fe)*

tive" Indian culture waiting to be celebrated in print and on canvas.

## The Art Colony Is Established

The "discovery" of Taos in 1898 by acclaimed artists Bert Greer Phillips and Ernest L. Blumenschein set off a chain of events that led to the establishment of Taos as a major art center, and other artists flocked into the area. Just after the turn of the century, Blumenschein and Phillips formed the Taos Society of Artists, inviting such masters as Walter Ufer, Victor Higgins, Joseph E. Sharp, E. Martin Hennings, and Oscar Berninghaus to join them. The other most famous members of the Taos Society include Catherine Carter Critcher, W. H. Dunton, and Kenneth Adams. The individual and collective contributions of the society radically transformed southwestern art. Trained in leading art schools in the eastern United States and Europe, the Taos artists, who flourished from 1900 to World War II, adapted their brilliant impressionist palettes and expressionist sense of design to the spectacular landscape of northern New Mexico and the "exotic" cultures of the Native Americans and Spanish colonists.

The arrival of more and more artists in Santa Fe and Taos stimulated interest in New Mexico's indigenous architecture. The New Mexico Museum of Fine Arts, built next to the plaza in 1914–1915, became a monument to the new Santa Fe style. "The Soul of the Southwest," a show of thirty-five paintings of Indians in their everyday surroundings by Walter Ufer, opened in the new museum on December 4, 1915. One month later, portrait painter Gerald Cassidy exhibited. By 1916, a small group of artists, including Cassidy, Carlos Vierra, Sheldon Parsons, and Robert Henri, were exhibiting their works together.

In April 1916, artist William Penhallow Henderson and his wife, internationally known poet Alice Corbin, moved to Santa Fe from

Boston. She persuaded poets such as Carl Sandburg, Vachel Lindsay, John Gould Fletcher, and Witter Bynner to visit Santa Fe. The Hendersons settled on Camino del Monte Sol. By 1921, potter Frank G. Applegate and Los Cinco Pintores (The Five Painters)—Will Shuster, J. G. Bakos, Fremont Ellis, Willard Nash, and Walter Mruk—became neighbors of the Hendersons in the sun-drenched foothills above Santa Fe. In contrast to the more traditional members of the Taos Society of Artists, Los Cinco Pintores were younger men inspired by modernism. Though intellectually espousing the ideals of abstraction, these artists actually painted in a variety of styles, a fact illustrative of the effect Santa Fe has in turning hard-line art theory into indefinable organic expression.

The expressionist and impressionist approaches to painting continue to influence artists' perceptions of New Mexico. Contemporary masterworks by New Mexican artists, such as Elmer Schooley's awesome pointillist-inspired landscapes, Robert Daughters's brilliant landscapes in a Van Gogh style, or David Barbero's highly charged canvases, evocative of André Derain, dominate Santa Fe's leading galleries. Great Native American painters have fully exploited the dramatic design and psychological potential of expressionism, as exemplified by the work of Fritz Scholder and John Nieto.

Georgia O'Keeffe's sensual paintings of New Mexico, endowed with muted and elegant color and a meditative quality, were perhaps the first to depict the landscape as a mysterious, spiritual, and sexual creative source. Married to photographer Alfred Stieglitz, O'Keeffe began in 1929 to take her summer vacations in New Mexico. Of course, through her association with Stieglitz, O'Keeffe knew many of the prominent New York artists of the 1920s and 1930s. New Mexico was a refreshing stimulus to O'Keeffe's art, and O'Keeffe was a welcome presence in New Mexico. Her arrival heralded the next great migration of artists and

72. *(Opposite page)* BY THE RIVER'S EDGE, *oil on canvas, by Victor Higgins (1884–1949). Victor Higgins arrived in New Mexico in 1913 and settled in Taos, where he even ran for mayor, losing the election by twelve votes. Higgins espoused a direct painting style of heavy, fluid brushstrokes and advocated that an artist build the "structure" of a painting as an architect carefully constructs a building. (Courtesy Zaplin-Lampert Gallery, Santa Fe)*

73. *(Opposite page)* OVERLOOKING THE RIO GRANDE, *oil on canvas, by Oscar Berninghaus (1874–1952). Largely self-taught, Oscar Berninghaus alternated spending seasons in St. Louis and Taos between 1893 and 1925. St. Louis collectors avidly supported his pictures of Indians, and Berninghaus found excellent subjects for his portraits among the residents of Taos Pueblo. (Courtesy Zaplin-Lampert Gallery, Santa Fe)*

74. NAVAJO WOMAN AND HORSE, *Olive Rush, oil on canvas. After moving to Santa Fe in 1920, Rush became well known for her paintings and frescos and for her work with young Indian artists, whom she encouraged to work with their own subject matter in a style natural to their culture. Her own work, which was influenced by Chinese painting, proceeds from an impulse that is intuitive and spiritual rather than directly visual. (Photograph by Marcia Keegan; courtesy Letta Wofford)*

75.  ACEQUIA MADRE, *oil on board, by Fremont Ellis (1897–1985).  A founding member of "Los Cinco Pintores," the Five Painters, Ellis displays masterful impressionistic technique and impressive powers of observation in this oil sketch of old Santa Fe.  (Courtesy Zaplin-Lampert Gallery, Santa Fe)*

CHURCH - RANCHOS DE TAOS

*Gustave Baumann*

76. RANCHOS DE TAOS CHURCH, *wood-cut, by Gustave Baumann (1881–1971). Baumann is best known for his luminous wood-block prints, many of favorite New Mexican subjects such as the famous mission church at Ranchos de Taos. (Courtesy Zaplin-Lampert Gallery, Santa Fe)*

77. END OF THE SNAKE DANCE, *oil,
Leon Gaspard (1882–1964). Russian
artist Leon Gaspard settled in Taos for
health reasons in 1918. Making Taos
his home for the rest of his life, Gaspard
traveled extensively around the world in
search of the exotic and picturesque. The
Snake Dance, a spectacular Hopi ceremonial, is seen here being enjoyed by a
partly Navajo audience. (Courtesy Museum of Fine Arts, Santa Fe)*

78. HOLLYHOCK PINK WITH PEDERNAL, *oil on canvas, Georgia O'Keeffe.* "*There has been no rain since I came out but today a little came—enough to wet the sage and moisten the top of the dry soil— and make the world smell very fresh and fine—I drove up the canyon four or five miles when the sun was low and I wish I could send you a mariposa lily—and the smell of the damp sage—the odd dark and bright look that comes over my world in the low light after a little rain—it is as still as can be. . . .*"

writers to the high country of the Sangre de Cristo Mountains.

D. H. Lawrence began his residency in Taos in 1920, making friends quickly with Mabel Dodge Luhan, a well-known hostess and supporter of Santa Fe's literary and artistic talents. Traveling with Lawrence were his wife Frieda and Dorothy Brett, an Englishwoman whose career as a painter was already well established abroad and who found new inspiration for abstracted genre scenes in New Mexico's people and places. Also attracted by New Mexico's extraordinary light and ancient cultures were photographers like Laura Gilpin, Ansel Adams, Edward Weston, and Paul Strand, who arrived in the 1930s and produced work that is today among the world's most collectible photography. A few of the other brilliant creative people who exploited southwestern themes in their works were writer Willa Cather and painters Andrew Dasburg, John Marin, Edward Hopper, Marsden Hartley, Leon Gaspard, and Nicolai Fechin.

While O'Keeffe's presence in New Mexico and the undisputed appeal of the Taos School began to attract widespread attention in the art world, Santa Fe became intent on re-creating its past. Between World War I and the Great Depression, the Santa Fe art colony had in fact become the city's most effective political lobbying group. The preservation of Santa Fe's style and culture was no longer a sentimental notion but a well-financed project. Between the two world wars, Victorian buildings on the plaza were transformed into Pueblo revival and territorial-style mercantile houses. In addition, the romantic cowboy style epitomized by Frederic Remington's heroic paintings became a vital part of the Santa Fe mystique. Western and Native American art are the bedrock of Santa Fe's art economy and reputation.

With such a teeming intellectual community in Santa Fe before the Depression, it is not surprising that many of the city's leading cul-

tural institutions and organizations were formed during this period. In September 1922, the First Annual Southwestern Indian Fair was successfully promoted to exhibit and sell Southwest Indian arts and crafts. Now called the Santa Fe Indian Market, it is the largest Indian market in the world and attracts over 100,000 visitors. During the a three-day extravaganza, an estimated $150 million is spent on art, accommodations, and entertainment.

Also in 1922, a group of people became concerned with the dangerous deterioration of the colonial churches. Anne Evans of Colorado spearheaded efforts to save them. Others involved included Mary Austin, Dan Kelly, the painter Carlos Vierra, and the architect John Gaw Meem. The group undertook a new building project each summer, often reroofing churches and replastering their crumbling adobe exteriors. Some of the committee's more spectacular successes included a major repair program at the famous Acoma mission and the purchase in 1929 of the Santuario de Chimayó, one of New

79. *Lady Dorothy Brett in her home in Taos. Lady Brett was a close associate of D. H. Lawrence, who spent time in Taos during the 1920s. Born in London, Brett came to New Mexico in 1924 with D. H. Lawrence, becoming an important part of his charmed circle of friends, along with Mabel Dodge Luhan. Brett remained a resident of Taos until her death in 1977. Brett's art evolved from portrait painting to sensitive pictures of Indians and their ceremonials. (Photograph by Marcia Keegan)*

Mexico's most beloved and best-preserved churches. The Santuario (whose foundation soil is believed to possess miraculous curative power) was later presented to the Archdiocese of Santa Fe with guarantees for its upkeep and maintenance. In 1932, the group was incorporated as the Society for the Preservation and Restoration of New Mexico Mission Churches. Though no longer active, the committee through its pioneer work, still serves as a model for the endless preservation efforts required for the churches. In 1987, Archbishop of Santa Fe Robert Sanchez created the Commission for the Preservation of New Mexico's Historic Churches, whose goals are similar to those championed in the 1920s.

As the renaissance in art and architecture matured, other aesthetic realms became ripe for revival. Under the influence of ceramicist Frank Applegate, who first came to New Mexico in 1921, and writer Mary Austin, traditional Hispanic arts and crafts began to gain attention. Applegate dreamed of a crafts revival similar to the arts and crafts movement led by William Morris at the end of the nineteenth century that revolutionized English and American design.

Spanish colonial arts and crafts in New Mexico were largely ignored in the Pueblo revival of the 1920s. Applegate, however, instantly recognized the integrity and intrinsic beauty of the Spanish religious art of New Mexico. By 1925, Austin and Applegate organized the Society for the Revival of Spanish Colonial Arts, later incorporated as the Spanish Colonial Arts Society. Still a vital part of Santa Fe's cultural milieu, the Spanish Colonial Arts Society organizes the annual Spanish Market each July and promotes traditional and contemporary work by New Mexico's Hispanic artists and craftspeople.

In this century southwestern American Indian art has ascended to the highest levels of quality and innovation and continues to produce recognized superstars. By the 1920s and 1930s, the work of Hopi potter Nampeyo and

San Idelfonso potters Maria and Julian Martinez was actively collected by prestigious galleries and museums, who insisted that they sign their work. Taos painter Pop Chalee and Santa Clara Pueblo artist Pablita Velarde also pioneered a distinctive, delicate, and graceful style of painting.

A major development in Native American painting took root in the Studio School of Indian Painting established in 1932 at the Santa Fe Indian School by art teacher Dorothy Dunn. Under Dunn's tutelage, young Indian artists were encouraged to draw inspiration from their own heritage rather than imitate European models of realism and impressionism. The Santa Fe Indian School became nationally famous as as "art colony" and graduated many

*80. Andrew Dasburg. Andrew Dasburg arrived in New Mexico in 1916 at the invitation of Mabel Dodge Luhan. Schooled in European modernism and cubism, Dasburg interpreted New Mexico's landscapes and villages in a structured and analytical style. (Photograph by Marcia Keegan)*

*81. Laura Gilpin and San Ildefonso Pueblo potter Maria Martinez. Laura Gilpin (left) is best known for her sensitive and noble photographs of the Navajo people and their land. Maria Martinez is recognized as one of the twentieth century's most accomplished potters. (Photograph by Marcia Keegan)*

students who would become internationally known artists, including Pablita Velarde, Tonita Peña (San Ildefonso), Allan Houser (Apache), Joe H. Herrera (Cochiti), Geronima Montoya (San Juan), Pop Chalee (Taos), Popovi Da, Alfonso Roybal (San Ildefonso), Teofilo Tafoya (Santa Clara), José Rey Toledo (Jeméz), Harrison Begay (Navajo), Quincy Tahoma (Navajo), Andy Tsinnajannie (Navajo), Fred Kabotie (Hopi), and Oscar Howe (Sioux).

The forms, media, and imagery of Native American art have continued to evolve. Pioneering contemporary artists such as Fritz Scholder, T. C. Cannon, and R. C. Gorman have developed highly individual approaches to the Native American heritage, ranging from fluid, elegant treatments of traditional figures to a bold use of color and gut-wrenching imagery depicting the painful side of the Native American past. Younger artists are proving no less innovative in their interpretations of their culture and history.

*82. THE FIRST TWINS, gouache, 1959, by Pablita Velarde. The birth of twins is an auspicious event in Pueblo culture. Renowned Santa Clara Pueblo artist Pablita Velarde portrays the birth of the first twins below and the events of their lives above, including their growth into powerful koshares (sacred clowns) and defeat of an evil ruler with the divine assistance of kachinas. (Courtesy Pablita Velarde, Clear Light Publishers)*

## Rebirth in the 1960s

Since the countercultural revolution of the 1960s, new artists and proponents of a new aesthetic have been attracted to New Mexico, complementing the traditional aesthetic but also introducing a profound new vision. The new breed of visionary artists in New Mexico responds to the same elements of culture and landscape that appealed to the Taos School and Georgia O'Keeffe but produces artworks on surprising themes and with unusual materials.

Since the 1960s, a fundamental reassessment of women and their role in society has led to the growth of the feminist movement. Feminism in New Mexico has encouraged artistic expression by women artists, many of whom are inspired by Georgia O'Keeffe's life and art.

*83.* APACHE MOUNTAIN SPIRIT DANCER, *bronze, by Allan Houser. First gaining prominence as a painter, Apache artist Allan Houser has revealed powerful expression in his sculpture. Houser's work can embody fluid motion (as seen here) or an abstract, monumental quality achieved with sparse, elegant modeling. (Photograph by the author)*

*84.* BASKET DANCE, *gouache, by Tonita Peña. A pupil of Dorothy Dunn at the Santa Fe Indian School in the 1930s, San Ildefonso Pueblo artist Tonita Peña retains a sense of classic and symmetrical Pueblo design in her painting of the Basket Dance. (Courtesy Letta Wofford)*

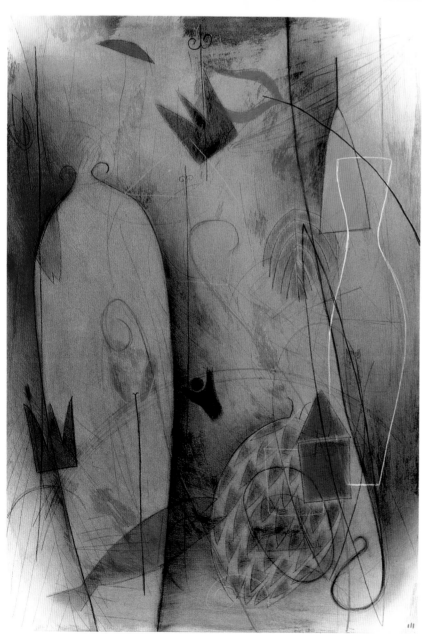

85. INDIAN MAIDEN, *acrylic on paper, by T. C. Cannon. In this painting, Cannon successfully exploits the flat, minimal design and bold color schemes which show the influence of French master Paul Gauguin. (Courtesy Zaplin-Lampert Gallery, Santa Fe)*

86. INVISIBLE, *paper on canvas with oil and other pigments, Emmi Whitehorse. Emmi Whitehorse's painting* Invisible *reveals sensuous plant forms along with other implied shapes and symbols, typical of the artist's enigmatic style. (Courtesy LewAllen Horwitch Gallery, Santa Fe)*

87. COLORADO, *lithograph, by R. C. Gorman. Gorman's images celebrate Navajo women as a source of nurturing, beauty, and nobility. The landscape and other elements in the picture, such as pottery, plants, and the sky are rendered to emphasize the compelling power of the human presence. (Courtesy the Navajo Gallery, Taos)*

Strong feminine roles existed in New Mexican culture long before the modern era. Pueblo women worked alongside men crafting pottery, weaving, and helping with the architectural maintenance of houses. Pueblo women have enjoyed a vital role in ceremonial rituals and dances. In the twentieth century, perhaps even more than the men, Pueblo women have risen to fame and critical acclaim as artists. Potters Maria Martinez, Sarafina and Margaret Tafoya, and Lucy Lewis and painters Pablita Velarde and Pop Chalee are just a few of the outstanding Pueblo women who have thrived within traditional cultural and sexual roles.

Navajo women have been recognized as world-class weavers for over a hundred years. Their powerful position in Navajo culture is underscored by the fact that family descent is determined by the mother and her clan and that the mother or wife owns the family's home. In the 1990s, Navajo women are successfully breaking new ground professionally, culturally, and socially. Artist Emmi Whitehorse is dazzling the southwestern art scene with her modernist-inspired canvases, full of elegant color compositions and abstract visual forms seemingly borrowed from a wide range of references. Whitehorse's canvases evoke the mythology of petroglyphs and personal symbols in a spirit reminiscent of Chagall and draw from the abstract sensibilities of modern masters such as Miro and Klee.

The parallel rise of feminism and the Chicano power movement since 1965 has caused deep changes in Hispanic and Mexican society across the southwestern United States. Triumphant cultural symbols and role models, such as the Virgin of Guadalupe and Mexican cult figure and artist Frida Kahlo, have inspired both men and women to reassess their roles and relationships. While painful, and sometimes tragic, the tension between the sexes in New Mexico's Hispanic culture has spawned a renaissance of creative activity.

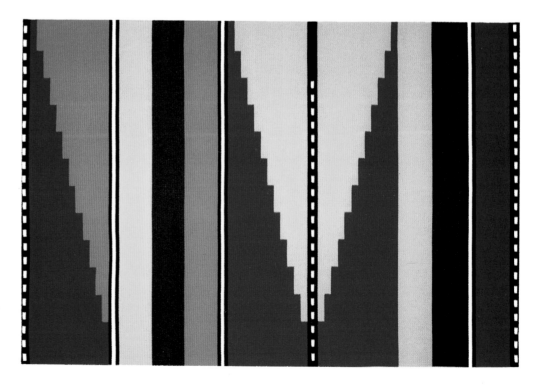

88. (Opposite page) DREAM STATE SERIES #14, *acrylic on canvas, by Dan Namingha. Contemporary Hopi artist Dan Namingha juxtaposes elements of kachina imagery and symbolism in his work. (Courtesy Niman Fine Art, Santa Fe)*

89. (Opposite page) BASKET DANCE/11, *weaving, 1991, by Ramona Sakiestewa. Hopi weaver Ramona Sakiestewa has revealed a personal and elegant sense of modern design in her tapestries, while drawing upon traditional Pueblo design motifs for inspiration. (Photograph by H. Lotz, courtesy the artist)*

90. NETI NETI, *collage, by Carlos Kemm. Assembled and manipulated images give Carlos Kemm's collages a complex and enigmatic quality. A young beauty is seduced by death beneath a water-like surface in this allegory of life and death. (Courtesy LewAllen Horwitch Gallery, Santa Fe)*

91. VAQUERO, *fiberglass sculpture by Luis Jimenez. Luis Jimenez's monumental sculpture of a Mexican vaquero, or cowboy, greets visitors to the National Museum of American Art in Washington, D. C. Jimenez's art combines the symbols of popular southwestern culture with dramatic imagery and unusual materials such as fiberglass and neon. (Photograph by the author)*

92. ALWAYS RETURNING, *acrylic on canvas, by Darren Vigil Gray. Apache artist Darren Vigil Gray's work employs painterly effects and a bold palette, along with Indian symbolism and subconscious imagery. (Courtesy Peyton-Wright Gallery, Santa Fe)*

93. CEREMONY, *oil on canvas, by Gary Yazzie. Navajo artist Gary Yazzie's paintings feature fluid brushwork and a bold color palette influenced by the French impressionists. (Courtesy ShiMa Traders, Gallup)*

94. LA PROCESSION DE LA VIRGEN DE GUADALUPE, *oil on canvas, Bernadette Vigil, 1991. The virgin of Guadalupe still retains an overwhelming devoted following among people of Hispanic descent in the Americas, including New Mexico. Bernadette Vigil has gained recognition among Hispanic artists for her powerful and moving paintings of everyday life in northern New Mexico, often combining an unusual perspective or vantage point with expressionistic colors.(Courtesy Owings-Dewey Fine Art, Santa Fe)*

Thus, New Mexico and its women possess a strength and appeal made mature by centuries of artistic expression. Within the past two decades, however, a major development in the Santa Fe art scene has been the remarkable increase in the prominence of women artists, especially minority women.

Another development that is increasingly influencing Santa Fe art is a mystical reverence for nature, which has long found expression in Native American art. This theme inspires the works of new Santa Fe visionaries such as Diana Bryer, Carol Bowles, and Douglas Johnson. As concern over the environment deepens, the work of these artists constitutes a profound expression of nature's spirit and power—the vital wellspring of the Santa Fe fantasy.

New Mexico's primitive but superbly elegant adobe architecture is being subtly sculpted and reinterpreted by artists such as interior designer James Jareb and neon artist Jan Sanchez. Jareb has successfully realized his own Santa Fe fantasy, a Moroccan-Santa Fe style house replete with bold wall colors and painted African designs. Jan Sanchez creates impressive adobe and neon "cities" in her art installations, juxtaposing primary shapes, such as cubes, spheres, and pyramids, to evoke memories of forsaken imperial capitals.

Raised within the Hispanic and Catholic tradition, Carlos Kemm, Cynthia Cook, Bernadette Vigil, Luis Tapia, Anita Rodríguez, and Rudy Fernández create profound and evocative images that conjure up paradoxical elements of the sacred and profane. Kemm's work, born of the symbolist and surrealist traditions, reflects the artist's own exploration of the subconscious and superconscious worlds. Cook's innovative tin frames surround traditional Catholic images of the saints in a personal, postmodern gothic style. Rudy Fernández has developed a highly personal visual language that bridges painting and sculpture, incorporating interesting art materials such as lead and neon. Familiar south-

western imagery such as roosters, trout, and cactus are given deep personal and psychological symbolic meaning in Fernández's work, cloaking the artist's raw emotion with color.

Romantic and fantastic images of preconquest southwestern culture pervade the watercolors of Douglas Johnson and Carol Bowles. In their visions of Pueblo and Native American life, the spiritual is made tangible, as if it was another pictorial element of the picture, as omnipresent as the sky, the sun, and nature.

A new type of renaissance is flourishing in

95. YELLOW ASPENS ABOVE SKI VALLEY, *oil on linen, by Alyce Frank. The alpine forests above Santa Fe provide Alyce Frank with a theme to practice her expressionistic response to design, color, and nature. (Courtesy Zaplin-Lampert Gallery, Santa Fe)*

Santa Fe in the 1990s. The artistic traditions of Anglo-Americans, Chicano and Mexican-Americans, and Native Americans are being drawn upon by all groups of artists for inspiration. While many artists follow a "purist" path, richly mining the wealth of their own cultural traditions, others consider the entire artistic tradition of New Mexico as fair territory for source material.

Thus, Pueblo painters express their visions with high-tech materials, Anglo artists remain fascinated with Hispanic and Native American subjects, and cutting-edge Chicano artists explore a world of magic realism and surrealism. The trading of ideas and artistic techniques across cultural frontiers is a relatively new phenomenon in New Mexico, one that promises to result in much more fantastic and "visionary" art. The artistic traditions and innovations of New Mexico continue to constitute an important aspect of the Santa Fe fantasy.

*96.* SUNDOWN, *oil on canvas, by Elmer Schooley. Elmer Schooley creates monumental landscapes by his unflinching attention to minute detail, an elegant feel for seasonal color influenced by French artist Pierre Bonnard, and an unusual appreciation for the ordinary aspects of nature. (Courtesy Munson Gallery, Santa Fe)*

# THE SPIRITUAL DIMENSION

Only a few regions in the world can boast an unbroken tradition of spiritual ceremonialism to match that of northern New Mexico. The thousand-year-old ritual dances and cosmological beliefs of the Ancient Ones still reverberate today in the villages of their descendants, the Hopi, Zuñi, and Rio Grande Pueblo Indians. The great kivas of Chaco Canyon, subterranean spiritual chambers carved out of the earth at least eight centuries ago, resound mightily in their windswept silence.

Over a period of six or seven centuries, the Navajos have also developed a complex ceremonial and religious culture. Ritual chants, songs, and dances help the People maintain harmony and balance with the universe. Sweat lodges are still frequently built across New Mexico to purify the body and spirit.

Attracted by a haunting landscape, rich in associations with ancient Indian civilizations and drawn too, some would say, by the intense magnetism of New Mexico's psychic energies, practitioners of a wide variety of spiritual beliefs have found their homes here as well. The Santa Fe area is home to Catholics, Protestants, Buddhists, Sikhs, Muslims, and a colorful variety of New Age practitioners, teachers, and spiritual guides. Tourists who visit New Mexico can partake of a feast of spiritual inspiration ranging from the ruins of the Ancient Ones to the offerings of the Age of Aquarius.

*97. (Opposite page) Altar, Santuario de Chimayó. The altar, reredo, of the Santuario, recently restored to its original intensity, is believed to be the work of Molleno, the "Chili Painter." (Photograph by Marcia Keegan)*

## The Kiva: Womb of the Pueblo Spirit

In Chaco Canyon, tourists and architectural students marvel at the vast stone mantra and meditation chambers called kivas. Literally an earthen womb for frail human spirits to transcend mortal reality, the kiva is spiritual architecture of the highest level. Like the kiva of the Ancient Ones, the kiva of the present-day Pueblo Indians is a primal spiritual chamber. Its architecture and painted decor have evolved, but its basic form has remained constant.

## Evolution of the Kiva

Creating shelter out of the earth itself—out of dried mud, logs, and other organic material—is a venerable practice going back thousands of

years. Indeed, some of the world's earliest structures and cities, many located in ancient Mesopotamia and Egypt, were constructed of adobe. It is not surprising then that the southwestern tribes now referred to as the Anasazi and Hohokam discovered that adobe was a building material perfectly suited to their dry, high desert environment.

The earliest pit houses were dark and smoky womblike structures that served both the spiritual and residential needs of the early indigenous peoples. Near the center of the floor, a small symbolic spirit hole, or *sipapu*, was dug to ensure a connection with benevolent natural spirits residing within the earth below. Natural *sipapu* are also believed to exist at secret, sacred places scattered throughout the southwestern homeland. In time, the pit house was adapted to become a kiva, a restricted ceremonial chamber where religious worship, chanting, dancing, and meditation take place.

Over the course of a millennium, the kiva has been developed by the Pueblo Indians into a simple, elegant, and beautiful architectural space of transcendent power. From small, circular clan kivas to the great kivas of the classic period of so-called Anasazi architecture (A.D. 1000–1275), the subterranean, rounded chambers have an uncanny effect on the human psyche. The geometric, circular dimensions of the room obscure human perceptions of space and distance. Sound and light are important architectural features of the kivas, attested to by the frequent presence of a firepit and foot drums. Within this man-made earth womb, heightened human consciousness is induced or coaxed forth as the mantra of chanting, pounding, rattling builds to a powerful crescendo.

The kiva is the heart of the ancient indigenous and modern Pueblo culture. Without the vital architectural and ceremonial link to the spiritual world, the People could not have endured the many trials of the past and withstood the hated Spaniards with their cruel religion and

others who came to steal and maim. As pure architectural form, the Pueblo kiva is unique in conception and construction. Examples of prehistoric kiva art have been preserved that indicate a previous Pueblo culture inspired by zoomorphic kachinas, divine creatures with the torso and legs of a human and the heads of various birds and animals. These powerful, perplexing images offer tantalizing insight into the wellspring of Pueblo artistic design, which still dominates the contemporary southwestern fine arts scene. The kiva architectural form was not adopted by later southwestern builders. Indeed, the Spanish friars used basic medieval and Renaissance Christian church forms in designing their church spaces and in many cases tried to destroy the Pueblo kivas.

### The Catholic Tradition

The kiva and Spanish mission construction form a perfect counterpoint of Old World and New World architecture, exemplifying the aspirations of the southwestern lifestyle and symbolizing the unspoken appeal of New Mexico.

*98. (Opposite page) Buffalo dancers, Nambé Pueblo. Nambé Pueblo's spectacular kiva provides an unforgettable stage for the emergence of buffalo dancers. (Photograph by Marcia Keegan)*

*99. Buffalo Dance, San Ildefonso Pueblo. The modern Pueblo communities perpetuate the centuries-old tradition of celebrating sacred animals such as the buffalo in their dance ceremonies. (Photograph by Marcia Keegan)*

Grounded in the earth, sensitive to the powerful forces of nature, in tune with natural rhythms, the kiva is a space of introspection and yet also of communal ritual. Defiant and soaring, the Spanish mission church is a triumph of the human will—of a community effort of survival. As its towers yearn skyward, it symbolizes our primordial desire to declare ourselves creatures of God, transcendent over nature.

The Spaniards brought a devout Catholicism, hardened by the Inquisition, to the New World. Missionary zeal accompanied by a lust for riches and power motivated the Spanish to colonize much of North and South America. After the failure of Coronado's expedition, the desire of the Church to save souls became the primary reason the northernmost province of Nuevo México was finally settled in 1598.

The clash of Pueblo religious ceremonialism and Catholic dogma produced many casualties —mostly Indian—but both religions have survived with remarkable strength and tenacity.

The Spanish colonists of New Mexico, due to severe isolation and lack of priests, evolved their own religious cult, the Penitente Brotherhood. Their *moradas*—small hybrid structures combining chapel and home—were built of adobe, wood, and stucco. In these places of spiritual retreat similar in function to kivas, the penitent *hermanos* (brothers) chant and pray. The *moradas* are adorned with beautifully carved wooden images of the saints (*santos*), wall plaques (*retablos*), simple carved furniture, and an altar at one end. Adorned with flowers and rosaries, the altars of *santos* are the Spanish equivalent of the Pueblo clan and prayer shrines blessed with carved figures, feathers, and offerings of cornmeal.

Rituals practiced by the Penitente Brotherhood, including self-flagellation, originated in the early Christian Church. During the first few centuries after Christ, the Desert Fathers retreated to the deserts of North Africa to renounce worldly temptations and practice a rig-

orous lifestyle of penance, physical hardship, fasts, and self-imposed physical punishments. From the earliest times, Christians were taught to celebrate Holy Week with masses, processions, and private observances of penance.

During the Middle Ages, orders of monks and nuns such as the Franciscans and the Dominicans began to flourish and continued the practice of self-flagellation as a form of penance. Mass public displays of self-flagellation were held during this period, especially at times of calamity, such as an earthquake or the Black Plague of 1347.

100. *Procession at Tome. Every year on Good Friday, hundreds of devoted Catholics climb El Cerro ("the hill") near Tome, south of Albuquerque, as a religious pilgrimage. Formed of volcanic rock, El Cerro provides a dramatic and spectacular setting for devotion and penance. (Photograph by Delilah Montoya)*

101. *(Opposite page) Chapel in Montezuma, New Mexico. Small village chapels abound in northern New Mexico, often displaying picturesque features such as folk art, camposantos (graveyards), and indigenous adobe architecture, like this chapel in Montezuma, five miles north of Las Vegas. (Photograph by Marcia Keegan)*

Because of its isolation and the long crusade against Islam, Spain preserved a somewhat fanatical and medieval Catholicism. In the sixteenth century, religious organizations and confraternities spread across Spain, including many which practiced self-flagellation during Holy Week. These observances were transported to the New World by the Spanish colonists. Gaspar Peréz de Villagrá, in his epic *Historia de La Nueva México*, describes the Holy Week ceremonies of the Oñate expedition in 1598. Juan de Oñate himself and other colonists "scourged their own shoulders with cruel blows, urgently praying for aid."

For many years outlying Spanish settlements in the territory were rarely visited by priests, and the Penitente Brotherhood played a vital role in maintaining the spiritual life of these communities. Penitente organizations have survived in New Mexico until the present day, but unfortunately have been the subject of much sensational and misleading publicity. The faith of the *hermanos* (brothers) and other traditional Hispanic Catholics remains a source of spiritual inspiration and has led to a resurgence of the *santero* tradition and other forms of religious folk art.

## A Spiritual Magnet for Many Beliefs

Well before Yankee Protestants arrived on the Santa Fe Trail, the Pueblo and other Native American people and the *hispaños* had already endowed the high country of New Mexico with a powerful spirituality. Centuries of chanting and praying, countless spectacular Pueblo dances, and the brooding, somber prayer rituals of the *hispaños* have permeated the Sangre de Cristo Mountains and the Rio Grande watershed with sacredness.

Since ancient times the earth in certain places in New Mexico has been considered sacred. *Sipapu* allow holy entities and spirits from the underground to join the human world. The

dirt at the Santuario de Chimayó, a classic colonial church, is widely thought to have healing powers. Thousands of believers make an annual pilgrimage to Chimayó during Holy Week preceding Easter Sunday. In addition, each Pueblo tribe has natural landmarks it considers sacred. Taos Pueblo reveres Blue Lake, the Zuñi tribe basks in the sun and shadow of Corn

*102. Sanctuary in the Santuario de Chimayó. Abandoned crutches, religious figures, keepsakes and other personal tokens of devotion line the walls of the healing sanctuary of the Santuario de Chimayó, a testament to the legendary healing powers of the church's soil. (Photograph by Marcia Keegan)*

103. Santuario, Chimayó. The Santuario de Chimayó beckons devoted worshipers to its inner sanctum, where sacred dirt is believed to heal physical and spiritual wounds. The name is adapted from the Indian name Tsimmayo. Native Americans first inhabited the Chimayó Valley between 1100 and 1400 and believed that on the site were healing spirits, connected with the warm, sulphurous springs. (Photograph by Marcia Keegan)

104. Pilgrimage to Chimayó. Each year during Semana Santa, or Holy Week, hundreds of faithful walkers converge on the Santuario de Chimayó to remember loved ones and give thanks for blessings and miracles conferred. (Photograph by Mark Nohl, courtesy New Mexico Magazine)

Mountain, and Acoma Pueblo atop a sheer cliff surveys Enchanted Mesa in the midst of an endless vista.

In the 1960s, dozens of young people, refugees from a confused and chaotic world, found refuge in several communes in the mountains of northern New Mexico. These self-sufficient communities became the seed of an alternative lifestyle movement that is rapidly maturing in and around Santa Fe.

Nurtured through the 1970s on the "exotic" mystical teachings of Yaqui shaman Don Juan in Carlos Castañeda's series of books, millions of people across the country began to question the purpose of a purely materialistic lifestyle. In addition, the psychospiritual adventures of

Harvard professors Timothy Leary and Richard Alpert motivated an entire generation of young Americans to "tune in and drop out." Alpert's transformation into Baba Ram Dass and his best-selling book *Be Here Now* inspired a movement and a migration to places such as Ojai, Aspen, Telluride, Taos, and Santa Fe in pursuit of a New Age lifestyle.

But the New Agers were not alone in their quest. Early in the 1970s, New Mexico also began to attract spiritual searchers with more traditional affiliations to the sacred Southwest. One of the earliest and best-known establishments was the Lama Foundation, a spiritual center near Taos with roots in several non-Western religious traditions, which has nur-

*105. Enchanted Mesa. Enchanted Mesa looms majestically across a vast valley from the famous Sky City of Ácoma Pueblo. The nearly perfect rock bluff is one of the treasured and sacred landmarks of the Pueblo landscape. (Photograph by Marcia Keegan)*

106. *The Sacred Blue Lake of Taos Pueblo. In 1971, after 60 years of struggle, Taos Pueblo was successful in its epic appeal to the U.S. government to reclaim its sacred Blue Lake from the Carson National Forest. Blue Lake is the site of religious pilgrimages and ceremonials performed at various times during the year and restricted to members of Taos Pueblo. (Taos Pueblo album photo)*

tured many residents and visitors over the past two decades. In 1973, Bodhi Mandala, a Zen Buddhist monastery was established near Jémez Springs. The healing hot waters of Jémez complement the ancient teachings of Rinzai Zen, a Japanese form of Buddhism. Between three and ten students practice meditation and chanting, eat at formal meals, and perform designated work activities, including gardening.

An original founder of the Lama Foundation, Abdullah Nuridin Durkee, converted to Islam in the early 1970s, and by 1979 he had developed plans for an Islamic community in New Mexico. His dream became reality. At a lovely site near Abiquiú, Dar Al-Islam has provided a haven for about thirty Sunni Moslem families from the United States and other countries, including Egypt, Turkey, Syria, Jordan, Spain, Great Britain, Holland, Belgium, and Ireland.

The same dramatic landscapes that enchanted Georgia O'Keeffe are a moving backdrop for the Mosque of Dar Al-Islam, designed and built by world-famous Egyptian architect Hassan Fathy. Here the adobe architecture of two great cultures, Islam and New Mexico, is joined harmoniously, much as the region's religious tolerance has made Dar Al-Islam an accepted part of the community.

Abiquiú in particular exemplifies the blend of cultures and spiritual aspirations that is one of the best qualities of New Mexico. Here, amidst awesome vistas of earth colored by an impressionist's paintbrush, several monasteries and retreats are flourishing. Besides Dar Al-Islam and, of course, the traditional Catholic communities of Abiquiú, El Rito, and Medanales, the Presbyterian Ghost Ranch property has provided sanctuary for many during its long history.

Also nearby is the Christ in the Desert Monastery. Santa Fe writer Jon Bowman has described the contemplative lifestyle at the isolated monastery:*

*Silence, prayer and austerity are also the order of the day at the Christ in the Desert Monastery, perhaps New Mexico's most remote spiritual enclave. A heavily rutted dirt road leads to a monastery in the red-rock country near Abiquiú. . . . Like the Benedictines in Pecos, the monks at Christ in the Desert welcome visitors, but the experience is much different. . . . The monastery offers no structural seminars or large retreats. It appeals to hardy individualists who trickle in one by one, looking for privacy and contemplation.*

*Guests must abide by the same stringent rules that apply to monks. Talking, for instance, is forbidden during meals. Instead, readings are recited from classic religious tomes. . . .*

*The physical setting of Christ in the Desert embodies its soul-searching mission. The silence is deafening, except for a chapel in the shadow of a rugged mesa. Overhead, a lone hawk spirals, riding the air currents. The Rio Chama flows down from the surrounding mountains, winding its way to the sea.*

*Jon Bowman, "Monastic Life Offers Refuge for Spiritual Seekers," *New Mexico* Magazine, March 1991, 32–34.

## Body, Mind, and Spirit

After 1980, Santa Fe and New Mexico became a magnet not only for a rapidly growing spiritual community but also for healers and psychic explorers of all persuasions. The influx of physical, psychological, and spiritual therapists tends to obscure the fact that the Pueblos, Navajos, and Hispanics have practiced natural and ritual medicine for hundreds of years. *Curanderismo*

(folk healing), shamanism, and other forms of healing that address the mind and spirit as well as the body are well established in New Mexico, even prominently featured in Rudolfo Anaya's landmark tale *Bless Me Ultima* and in Tony Hillerman's popular Navajo crime mysteries.

Hispanic folk medicine, or *curanderismo*, is based on a deep faith in the natural healing power of the land and its plants and herbs and also in the benevolent interaction of the patron saints of Catholicism. The *curandera* or *curandero* begins a treatment by interviewing the patient to determine the proper tea, ointment, or poultice to prepare.

Often, the *curandera* is familiar with the patient as a result of several generations of family acquaintanceship. The treatment prescribed usually includes prayers to a family or personal patron saint for divine assistance. This personal approach to healing is a centuries-old tradition in New Mexico, and *curanderas* are trained by a long apprenticeship with an acknowledged healer.

111. *Modern* curandera. *Elena Avila of Rio Rancho is a current practitioner of* curanderismo *and other natural healing arts in the Hispanic tradition. (Photograph by Delilah Montoya)*

This form of healing is widely accepted by many people and survives to this day.

Observers of the ancient capital cannot help but notice that, whatever else Santa Fe is, it has also become a capital of New Age culture. Today, the city is among the world's leading centers of the alternative health care and spiritual development movements. Thriving local stores specialize in books, herbs, and other products relating to alternative body and mind therapies, spirituality, and esoteric philosophy. Local phone books list practitioners of every imaginable therapy, and bulletin boards and newspapers are crammed with listings for workshops, classes, and spiritual counseling. Santa Fe annually hosts the Whole Life Expo, a three-day convention and fair that presents the entire gamut of New Age healing and lifestyle offerings. It is the world's largest meeting of practitioners of "health, fitness, and awareness of body, mind, and spirit."

Santa Fe offers an amazing diversity of approaches to personal growth and spiritual and physical healing. Classic Western psychothera-

pies such as Jungian analysis and psychosynthesis are available, together with opportunities to experience Eastern religious traditions, including Tibetan Buddhism, Zen Buddhism, Sufism, and Native American spirituality; the twentieth-century philosophical teachings of Gurdjieff and Ouspensky; and "traditional" occult systems such as tarot, I Ching, and astrology.

Several well-known schools provide accredited programs in body work and oriental medicine. These include New Mexico Academy of Healing Arts, Scherer's Academy of Natural Healing, International Institute of Chinese Medicine, and Southwest Acupuncture College. Masters degree programs in spiritually oriented counseling and art therapy are offered by Southwestern College, a local academic institution. Just south of Santa Fe is the Light Institute headed by Chris Griscom, whose work became nationally known after the publication of Shirley Maclaine's book *Dancing in the Light*. The institute focuses on consciousness development and past life therapy. Associated with the institute is the Nizhoni School for Global Consciousness, an international day and boarding school for children and adults.

Practitioners of spiritual and psychic counseling and healing, channeling, crystal healing, and shamanism are numerous. Other healing modalities for body, mind, and spirit include naturopathy, homeopathy, Reiki, shiatsu, t'ai chi, yoga, rebirthing, polarity work, aromatherapy, applied kinesiology, foot reflexology, nutritional counseling, and holotropic breath work. A number of well-known practitioners of alternative therapies work on animals on the physical and psychic levels. Typically Santa Fe healers and practitioners develop skills in more than one area, combining, for example, shamanism and psychotherapy, or chakra psychology with body work.

Commenting on the healing and growth movement in Santa Fe, one local practitioner observes that "the object is not to make a living.

The object is to change the world." He goes on to say that "the energy here has no tolerance for charlatans. Some do come here, but if you don't come here with a clear intent, Santa Fe has a way of asking you to leave."

Those who seek healing for body, mind, and spirit represent only a fraction of the influx of newcomers attracted to Santa Fe. Others are drawn by personal fantasies of enchantment—fantasies of the good life, closeness to nature, and exotic cultures that may bring an added dimension to their lives; fantasies of aesthetic inspiration and support for artistic strivings; and modern day fantasies harking back to the Seven Cities and fortunes that could be made. Despite its allure as a golden city, Santa Fe cannot and should not be all things to all people. The city's rapid growth in the past two decades taxes its natural resources, especially its water supply and the fragile high desert and mountain environment that is perhaps the ultimate source of its spiritual magic.

## The Old and the New

At the dawn of the 1990s, the Old World met the New with warnings and prayers of hope. In December 1990, Hopi spiritual leaders met New Mexico Governor-elect Bruce King to offer him their advice and prophecies. Political leaders must begin to work together, they said, to halt rampant mistreatment of Mother Earth or face dire consequences. Pollution, mining abuses, and deforestation of the land threaten the sacred homeland of the Ancient Ones.

Later, in April 1991, His Holiness the Dalai Lama visited New Mexico on a triumphant tour. One highlight of his visit was a private meeting with the governors and tribal members of New Mexico's pueblos that reaffirmed a deep spiritual affinity between the two cultures.

The blossoming of alternative lifestyles in New Mexico in the 1990s is perhaps a manifestation not only of spiritual renaissance but also

112. *Tibetan Buddhist stupa, Santa Fe. Construction was completed in the 1980s. At this Buddhist center, Kagyu Shenpen Kunchab, aspirants find an opportunity to study and practice Tibetan Buddhism under qualified teachers, as well as to study Tibetan language and culture. KSK also serves the growing number of Tibetan refugees living in Santa Fe. The stupa, or meditation hall, was built according to specifications laid out in a rare Buddhist text. (Photograph by Rob Lee; courtesy of KSK Buddhist Center)*

113. *Tibetan monks. Tibetan monks from the Gyuto Monastery perform a healing ceremony atop the Sandia Mountains over Albuquerque in 1992. (Photograph by Marcia Keegan)*

spiritual impoverishment. Many of us seek an ideal environment—a utopia untroubled by poverty, strife, and violence. New Mexico may provide a safe haven from some of those problems, but even the so-called Land of Enchantment has witnessed unspeakable acts of violence and warfare in its long history.

Part of what has been lost in modern life is a primal connection between people and the land, a catastrophe with dire consequences in the view of many Native Americans. In his state-

ment to Governor-elect Bruce King on December 13, 1990, Hopi elder Martin Gashweseoma spoke of Santa Fe's role as a forum for spiritual and political exchange:

*I am the keeper of the sacred Fire Clan tablet of the Hopi at the village of Hotevilla. This tablet represents our ancient title to this land, which has existed for many centuries before the arrival of Columbus, and has never been relinquished to this day. It has been entrusted to me under the highest authority, to be held until the last stage of our prophecies has been completed. The signs that we have entered the final phase are now clear...*

*The modern concept of land title does not hold the key to peace. Instead, because it is based on conquest, which is theft, it is the basic cause of the problems which now threaten to end life on earth. Hopi land title is based on permission. We received that permission from Maasaw, the guardian of all land and life, who holds it in trust from the Creator. Thus it is implemented by the forces that create the universe. Regardless of differences in culture and tradition, true aboriginal title throughout the world is based on a similar relationship. . . . The only hope for*

*humanity lies in restoring true land title, which is inseparable from our function as caretakers of life.*

*For this we bring our sacred stone tablets to the New Mexico state capital in Santa Fe. Because it is the first foreign capital on this land, there must be documents here that confirm the rights of the original native people, and possibly information regarding stone tablets such as those we brought with us. We want to see whether the original title of the native peoples, including the Hopi, is still binding according to existing modern laws.*

*The great powers of the modern world need to realize that if they are to escape the punishment that lies ahead, what they are doing to native peoples around the world must be corrected. Those who accumulate power at the expense of the native peoples think they have a God-given right, but in so doing they are increasing the threat to all life. And although they now recognize that threat, they are powerless to reverse it by any means unless they stop preying upon the native peoples.*

Martin Gashweseoma,
Hopi Elder
December 13, 1990

114. *Governor Bruce King and Pueblo priests. Pueblo priests and medicine men address their concerns for their sacred homeland to New Mexico Governor Bruce King in the State Capitol recently. (Photograph by Marcia Keegan)*

115. *Corn Mountain. Dowa Yalaane, the sacred "Corn Mountain" of Zuñi Pueblo, has provided a sacred refuge for the tribe for nearly 1,000 years. (Photograph by the author)*

# MODERN AND POSTMODERN

The modern era began in New Mexico with its "discovery" by artists, writers, and other intellectuals after 1900. By 1925, both Santa Fe and Taos boasted colonies of creative people and famous visitors who began to interpret New Mexico's people, landscape, and culture from an entirely new point of view. D. H. Lawrence experienced an "awakening" in his first encounter with the New Mexican landscape:

*I think New Mexico was the greatest experience from the outside world that I have ever had. It certainly changed me forever. Curious as it may sound, it was New Mexico that liberated me from the present era of civilization, the great era of material and mechanical development. Months spent in holy Kandy, in Ceylon, the holy of holies of Southern Buddhism, had not touched the great psyche of materialism and idealism which dominated me. And years, even in the exquisite beauty of Sicily, right among the old Greek paganism that still lives there, had not shattered the essential Christianity on which my character was established. Australia was sort of a dream or trance, like being under a spell, the self remaining unchanged, so long as the trance did not last too long. . . .*

*But the moment I saw the brilliant, proud morning shine high up over the deserts of Santa Fe, something stood still in my soul, and I started to attend. There was a certain magnificence in the high-up day, a certain eagle-like royalty.* *

*From "New Mexico," Phoenix: The Posthumous Papers of D. H. Lawrence by D. H. Lawrence and edited by Edward McDonald. Copyright 1936 by Frieda Lawrence, renewed © 1964 by The Estate of the late Frieda Lawrence Ravagli. Used by permission of Viking Penguin, a division of Penguin Books USA Inc.

Visiting New Mexico at about the same period, Carl Jung expressed his openness to learning from Indian wisdom:**

*On my next trip to the United States, I went with a group of American friends to visit the Indians of New Mexico, the city-building Pueblos. "City," however, is too strong a word. What they build are in reality only villages, but their crowded houses piled one atop the other suggest the word "city," as do their language and their whole manner. There for the first time I had the good fortune to talk with a non-European, that is, to a non-white. He was a chief of the Taos pueblos, an intelligent man between the ages of forty and fifty. His name was Ochwiay Biano (Mountain Lake). I was able to talk with him as I have rarely been able to talk to a European. To be sure, he was caught up in his world just as much as a European is in his, but what a world it was! In talk with a European, one is constantly running up on the sandbars of things long known but never understood; with this Indian, the vessel floated freely on deep, alien seas. At the same time, one never knows which is more enjoyable: catching sight of new shores, or discovering new approaches to age-old knowledge that has almost been forgotten.*

*"See," Ochwiay Biano said, "how cruel the whites look. Their lips are thin, their noses sharp, their faces*

116. CLOUDS, *photograph, by Eliot Porter. One of America's greatest landscape photographers, Porter captures the enigmatic quality of New Mexico skies in his "Clouds" series. (Museum of Fine Arts, Santa Fe)*

117. SANTA FE POSTMODERN, *casein on paper, by Douglas Johnson.*

*furrowed and distorted by folds. Their eyes have a staring expression; they are always seeking something. What are they seeking? The whites always want something; they are always uneasy and restless. We do not know what they want. We do not understand them. We think that they are mad."*

*I asked him why he thought whites were all mad.*

*"They say that they think with their heads," he replied.*

*"Why of course. What do you think with?" I asked him in surprise.*

*"We think here," he said, indicating his heart.\*\**

Nearly seven decades after D. H. Lawrence and C. G. Jung wrote their famous essays, perhaps some of the mystique they appreciated in the land and its people has been lost, sacrificed to the demands of development and tourism.

## The Postwar Period

Santa Fe and New Mexico have changed radically since the halcyon years of the 1920s and 1930s, having been discovered and rediscovered many times by successive waves of artists, writers, intellectuals, and other cultural immigrants.

During World War II, the defense industry invested heavily in New Mexico, building an entire top-secret community at Los Alamos and another sophisticated weapons and research facility called Sandia National Laboratories in Albuquerque. New Mexico abruptly entered the modern era, and Albuquerque boomed in classic American suburban style, complete with streamlined international-style housing developments.

World War II had other profound effects on New Mexico. The Spanish colonial arts and crafts revival, begun in the mid-1920s, was one significant casualty of the war, as young Hispanic New Mexican tinsmiths, weavers, and carpenters ventured to far-off corners of the

\* From *Memories, Dreams, Reflections* by C. G. Jung, rec. and ed. by Aniela Jaffe, trans. by R. and C. Winston. Translation copyright © 1961, 1962, 1963 by Random House, Inc. Reprinted by permission of Pantheon Books, a division of Random House, Inc.

globe to fight the Axis powers. Courageous young Native American men joined their Hispanic and Anglo comrades and served their country valiantly. The legendary Navajo Code Talkers baffled the Japanese communications network for three years and became one of the U.S. Marine Corps' most celebrated units.

While World War II had only limited physical effects on the sacred homeland of the Rio Grande, it had profound effects on the people directly or indirectly involved in fighting the war. Hispanic and Native American veterans were exposed to the world and to American values for the first time. They now wanted their children to succeed in the American mainstream and to aspire to experiences and success beyond the Southwest's friendly, secure landscape. Children were now raised speaking English, formal education was considered imperative for economic and social success, and the small villages and pueblos were abandoned by those seeking the American Dream.

After the war, Hispanic families began migrating to Albuquerque, Denver, El Paso, and other cities in search of jobs and a new start. The quaint old Spanish-style wooden furniture was

118. **PATROCINIO BARELA**, *oil on canvas, by Edward Gonzales. Noted contemporary Hispanic painter Edward Gonzales of Santa Fe credits santero Patrocinio Barela with being a major artistic influence. According to Gonzales, Barela transcended traditional folk art to become a true visionary artist. (Collection of Jeanne and Joseph Sullivan; courtesy Edward Gonzales)*

119. *Adobe home on Canyon Road. Canyon Road boasts some of Santa Fe's finest art galleries, restaurants, and classic houses. (Photograph by Marcia Keegan)*

120. *Territorial house on Canyon Road, Santa Fe. The U.S. Army introduced the territorial style to New Mexico at Fort Union and Fort Marcy after 1850. The Greek revival elements of the new style are seen on this Canyon Road house in the shuttered windows and brick coping pattern crowning the facade. (Photograph by Marcia Keegan)*

121. *Santa Fe Plaza. The obelisk in the center of Santa Fe's plaza marks the end of the Santa Fe Trail. During the summer season, the plaza hosts thousands of people to celebrate the Spanish Market (in July), the Indian Market (in August), and the Fiesta (in September). (Photograph by the author)*

122. *Museum of Fine Arts, Santa Fe. The Museum of Fine Arts on the plaza built in 1916–1917, was one of the first monuments of the Pueblo revival style. The architecture of Acoma's mission church of San Estevan was a major influence on the museum's form and massing. (Photograph by the author)*

put away, sold cheaply, or discarded in favor of Sears Roebuck sofas and easy chairs. In the 1950s, television began infiltrating even the most isolated homesteads, and the old culture of New Mexico was in danger of fading away.

Meanwhile, Santa Fe entered a brief span of complacency. Albuquerque's large military bases, the Los Alamos and Sandia nuclear facilities, and the dramatic growth of the University of New Mexico ensured the area's status as an emerging southwestern center.

The Eisenhower era witnessed the founding of the Santa Fe Opera and the Santa Fe and Taos Ski valleys in the mid-1950s, all three currently cornerstones of the state's tourist industry. During the formative years of the opera, the composer Igor Stravinsky's residency in Santa Fe won the young company instant recognition and a loyal following of devoted fans from throughout the United States. Similarly, Swiss ski entrepreneur Ernie Blake literally handcrafted Taos Ski Valley, in the late 1950s, now called the most "European" ski resort in America. With its heavenly light powder snow and expert-level trails, Taos has become a haven for the winter jet set. Both the ski valleys and the opera experienced growing pains through the early years. The opera gave performances in Sweeney Gymnasium in downtown Santa Fe before its magnificent open-air amphitheater was built on a hilltop overlooking the Rio Grande in 1965.

With the founding of the opera and the ski valleys, a new year-round group of sophisticated visitors began to discover the charms of northern New Mexico. Throughout the 1950s and 1960s, the style consciousness created by the pioneering Pueblo revival enthusiasts matured. Schools, commercial buildings, fast-food restaurants, and modestly priced tract homes in outlying neighborhoods of the capital city incorporated traditional design elements such as earth-colored stucco and projecting roof *vigas* (log beams) drawn from Pueblo architecture.

Gradually, too, the Santa Fe Plaza transformed its "American" storefronts to the southwestern look. In 1966, architect John Gaw Meem designed exterior Pueblo-style portals for three sides of the plaza, which now give the oldest part of Santa Fe a unified look. Meanwhile, in another part of Santa Fe, architect Peter Van Dresser was investigating the potential of solar energy to heat adobe homes. His house, built in 1958, was the forerunner of a solar housing movement that peaked in the 1970s and 1980s.

there after 1985: *Silverado, Lust in the Dust, Young Guns,* and *The Milagro Beanfield War.*

Santa Fe—its image, culture, and "style"—seem to have taken both the United States and Europe by storm. In New York, Honalulu, Paris, and other international cities, travelers report finding Santa Fe fashions and interior design, Santa Fe perfumes, soaps, and wines, Santa Fe restaurants and spas—even a "Santa Fe" yacht club in Hoboken, New Jersey.

*123. BOHR'S DOUBT, photograph, by Meridel Rubinstein. Santa Fe photographer Meridel Rubinstein's recent photographs utilize collage technique to express the ironic coincidence of northern New Mexico being the home of America's oldest native cultures and newest space age atomic technology (at Los Alamos National Laboratory). (Courtesy LewAllen HorwitchGallery, Santa Fe)*

*124. Gate, James Jareb House. North African and southwestern stylized "power animals" are painted onto the front wall of designer James Jareb's compound in Santa Fe. (Courtesy James Jareb)*

## The Santa Fe Boom

Though known for years among cultured travelers, wealthy opera patrons, collectors of fine art, and lovers of Indian arts and crafts, the enchantment of Santa Fe was not apparent to the rest of the world until *Esquire* magazine published a long essay on the Santa Fe lifestyle in 1981. The cover story, titled "The Right Place," exclaimed (from the male point of view): "We've found it: great women, great weather, and plenty to do. Pack your bags! You've always dreamed of living there—the great place where everything is going to be different."

Scores of other national magazines soon followed *Esquire's* lead and published their own feature articles on the charms of Santa Fe. Dandy Don Meredith, of Dallas Cowboy football fame, began boasting to cohost Frank Gifford about his off-season adobe hideaway in Santa Fe on ABC's "Monday Night Football" telecasts. Amy Irving and Steven Spielberg were married in Santa Fe. Irving had spent a couple of summers in the Santa Fe foothills with friends and had acted in small community theater productions to keep her skills sharp. Sam Shepard and Jessica Lange spent a romantic interlude in the Ancient City, where they could pal around seemingly unnoticed. Hollywood's romance with the Santa Fe area culminated in a rapid-fire succession of movies filmed near

## Postmodernism and Santa Fe Style

Interestingly, the growing visitor and residential appeal of Santa Fe coincided with changing currents in architecture and interior design. After the art deco movement of 1925–1935 was dismissed as overly decadent and frivolous, leading European designers, led by architects Le Corbusier, Walter Gropius, and the German Bauhaus school, began to strip away excess ornament and color from houses and furniture. In the 1930s, the use of rigid geometry, stark white interiors with chrome and leather "manufactured" furniture, and modern industrial materials such as glass block was espoused. The so-called "international style" reigned supreme in Europe and the United States well into the 1960s. The long dominance of the international style, at least in residential design, fostered and established a "modernist" aesthetic canon that was accepted by most designers and builders. The baby boom of the 1950s created a need for housing, and the suburbs, meeting the demands of the time, were soon filled with rows of boxy, uncluttered, modern houses.

In 1966, a brilliant young architect, Robert Venturi, articulated some of the growing unease with the modernist movement in his landmark book *Complexity and Contradiction in Architecture*. This book is now considered to have virtually launched the postmodern architectural movement of the 1970s, 1980s, and 1990s. The rise of postmodernism in America is at the root of the popularity of Santa Fe style and other stylistic revivals. Postmodernism encourages a reinvestigation of traditional historic styles, motifs, and entire "design languages" such as Renaissance classicism or Queen Anne. Designers are free to seek inspiration among historical design elements and reformulate them in contemporary and idiosyncratic ways. They make up their own rules, can juxtapose traditional and industrial materials at will, and may employ harmonies and proportions previously

proscribed by accepted rules of design. Thus, Charles Moore can adorn his classical composition of the Piazza d'Italia in New Orleans with bright neon tubing. Philip Johnson, building his towering New York skyscraper in 1984 for AT&T, crowned it with a Chippendale chair-inspired pediment. Though modernism has not been completely supplanted by postmodernism, by 1980 architects and designers were scouring the design closets of history in search of new ideas.

Furniture design followed closely on the heels of the architectural new wave. The furniture of the international style was meant to look as if human hands had not been involved in constructing it. Clean, streamlined design; angular, geometric composition; and modern chrome and leather materials produced sleek, handsome-looking furniture with no references to the past. The technology of home appliances—televisions, washing machines, and microwave ovens—has continuously advanced, and a high-tech aesthetic is accepted as appropriate for them. Increasingly, though, traditional objects of comfort and convenience, such as sofas, easy chairs, cupboards, and chests of drawers, offer tremendous appeal when built in recognizable historic styles. Homeowners now want the best of both worlds: flashy high-tech appliances, computers, and electronic equipment hidden away in furniture that would look at home in a Norman Rockwell painting.

In fact, the 1980s and 1990s have seen a resurgence in traditional and nostalgic styles. *Metropolitan Home* magazine, Ralph Lauren, and Terence Conran understand this phenomenon and have expertly exploited its marketing potential. After the austerity of the modernist aesthetic, people are hungering for color, interesting textures, hand-rubbed finishes, and skilled craftmanship. Santa Fe style merchandise has all of these qualities and more to offer. Collectors and dealers have scoured the Southwest and Mexico hunting for furniture and decorative arts of timeless and authentic appeal. The 1990s will continue to seek a balance between the machine-age aesthetic that has dominated the twentieth century and the handcrafted, humanist products that are now in high demand.

## Postmodernism and the Southwestern Lifestyle Frontier

In the 1990s, Santa Fe and the Southwest promise a new Santa Fe fantasy, a unique lifestyle frontier that combines the traditional cultural elements developed over many centuries with the most innovative and trendy technological developments.

Postmodernism, as it affects the 1990s in the Southwest, involves the modification of historically established styles, techniques, traditions, and beliefs by contemporary methods, technology, and sensibilities. Cross-cultural and cross-regional pollinization of ideas is characteristic of postmodernism, as is cross-temporal expres-

125. (Opposite page) Greene/Nathanson House, Albuquerque, Bob Heiser, architect, DCSW Architects of Albuquerque. The house displays Mediterranean influences from the Greek isles and southwestern massing in its multifaceted facades. (Courtesy DCSW Architects)

126. (Opposite page) The Beach Apartment Complex, Antoine Predock, architect. An early example of contemporary southwestern regionalism on Albuquerque's historic Route 66. Inspired by the cubical massing of Pueblo apartment complexes such as Taos Pueblo, Predock chooses a jazzy color scheme and neon accents to create a neowestern image. (Photograph by the author)

127. (Opposite page) Peralta Complex, Santa Fe. Recent commercial architecture in Santa Fe embraces the streamlined modernist aesthetic but retains a New Mexican color palette. (Photograph by the author)

128. Colonial bed, Ramón José López. Santero Ramón José López won a top prize at the 1993 Spanish Market for this piece. Images of popular New Mexican saints adorn the head- and footboards, and all pigments are natural. (Courtesy Ramón José López)

sion—the combining of ideas from the past and the present.

If a postmodern sensibility is dawning in the world, then surely it is raging in Santa Fe. Postmodernism is being expressed at an accelerated rate in the Southwest's architecture, interior design, fashion, and related decorative arts. Postmodernism is also at work in New Mexico culture in its cuisine, music, spiritual life, art, and literature. The sheer influx of architects and designers attracted by the boom in southwestern style has caused a new renaissance of unprecedented proportions.

Southwestern architecture is currently being redefined and reinvented along several parallel modes: the Pueblo style, the Spanish colonial revival, the territorial, ranch, or cowboy style, the mission style, the Pueblo deco style, and postmodernism itself.

Breaking from the powerful tradition of Pueblo revival architecture, which has been a dominant force in New Mexican architecture since 1920, has given rise to a less "purist" more eclectic spirit. Prominent New Mexico designers such as Bart Prince, Antoine Predock, Ed Mazria, Westwork Architects, and Design Collaborative Southwest have introduced new styles and combinations of old and new styles to the southwestern architectural tradition. New materials and technologies, including solar housing, form part of a growing environmentally friendly trend in architecture. Other influences can be traced to modern giants of architecture such as Le Corbusier, Bruce Goff, or Luis Barragán. Many designers are exploiting the potential of fusing international traditions with southwestern forms.

Within the many vast design languages developed over centuries in the Southwest lies a wealth of inspiration. Designers such as cowboy furniture maker L. D. Burke III have successfully bridged the past and present. Burke's translation of the timeless, primitive appeal and mortise-and-tenon joinery of the Hispanic

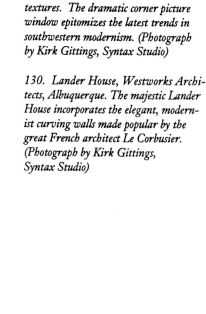

129. (Above) Anderson House, Albuquerque, John Anderson, architect. Anderson's house in Albuquerque fuses the sleek geometry of the modernist aesthetic with traditional materials and textures. The dramatic corner picture window epitomizes the latest trends in southwestern modernism. (Photograph by Kirk Gittings, Syntax Studio)

130. Lander House, Westworks Architects, Albuquerque. The majestic Lander House incorporates the elegant, modernist curving walls made popular by the great French architect Le Corbusier. (Photograph by Kirk Gittings, Syntax Studio)

forms into his own dramatic cowboy furniture is an established "postmodern" southwestern legend.

Sought by movie stars, presidents, and many other collectors, Burke's pieces often boast commonsense "cowboy wisdom," sayings pounded out meticulously in nails on cabinets and mirrors. Among his favorite sayings are: "Cows to tend, money to lend, all 'mounts to nothing, without a good friend"; or "If you want to get there, ride one horse at a time."

Burke operates his furniture enterprise out of a unique structure of his design, affectionately called the "Pink Church" by friends and neighbors. A postmodern interpretation of common New Mexican mission church forms, the Burke studio marries the best of traditional New Mexican architectural imagery with the industrial functionalism of the 1990s.

In true Burke (and Santa Fe) fashion, he claims to have "channeled" the design for the studio. "It came to me all in one vision. I sat down and did the working drawings in one afternoon. Yep, I channeled that darn thing. And you can print that."

An example of postmodern residential architecture is the Greene/Nathanson house, designed by architect Bob Heiser of Design Collaborative Southwest. The house includes references to New Mexico's traditional architecture in form and massing but breaks away to explore international influences. According to Heiser, the owner's inspiration grew from trips and periods of residence in the Greek isles; therefore the term "Mikonos modern" seems appropriate. The central dome recalls Islamic and Middle Eastern buildings, and the color accents remind one of the dramatic palette for walls developed by Mexico's master architect Luis Barragán. The stretching of "adobe" architectural parameters to include international stylistic references and new technological capabilities is a notable innovation in New Mexico architecture in the late twentieth century.

131. Lander House, detail, Westwork Architects, Albuquerque. A pristine natural site near Albuquerque complements the complex geometry of the Lander House. (Photograph by Kirk Gittings, Syntax Studio)

132. Friedman House, Westwork Architects, Albuquerque. The planar abstractions and juxtapositions of Westwork Architects' Friedman House in Albuquerque recall the early modernist compositions of the cubist artists, only here in full three dimensions beneath the Sandia Mountains. (Photograph by Kirk Gittings, Syntax Studio)

133. Pink Church on Pacheco Street, Santa Fe, L. D. Burke III, architect. Burke's studio and furniture showroom is a neo-mission-style elaboration of a New Mexican church facade employing industrial materials. (Photograph by Lindsay Holt; courtesy L. D. Burke III)

Another postmodern design phenomenon that has sprung up in northern New Mexico might be termed "alternative housing" or "folk architecture." A number of artists and visionaries are creating houses and other structures that are unique personal expressions, works in progress that are not built to be sold and take many years, perhaps even a lifetime, to complete. They are built around an unusual concept, site, or materials. One example is Ross and Carla Ward's Tinkertown Museum in Sandia Park, which is enclosed within walls composed chiefly of over 40,000 empty bottles. Construction began well before recycling became an issue of concern. The walls, which are twelve to fifteen inches thick, allow distinctive natural illumination—sunlight sparkling through multicolored glass. The museum houses "an amazing, animated, miniature wood-carved western town and circus" that Ross Ward has been hand-carving since 1962.

Artist Douglas Johnson has been creating his house for twenty years. Based on the "ancestral Pueblo" design of Chaco Canyon, it is built into a natural rock formation on the side of a cliff. The primary materials Johnson uses are sandstone and cement accented with bands of smooth river rock.

Another New Mexico artist, Mark Rendleman, is creating a maze of tunnels and caves in a mountain near the Rio Grande. Carved out of a soft, sandstone-like material, the structure is lighted naturally by skylights, windows, and reflecting mirrors and serves as a gallery for the artist's collection of art and artifacts.

Innovations in environmentally conscious housing include actor Dennis Weaver's 100 percent solar "Earth Ship," a southwestern-style house in Taos designed by Mike Reynolds, of Solar Survival Architecture, with walls constructed of automobile tires and beer or soda cans plastered over with adobe. With Earth Ship, Reynolds has created a generic model for low-tech, low-maintenance, affordable housing

*134. Entry Doors, Inn of the Anasazi, Jeremy Morrelli. Master craftsman Jeremy Morrelli's distinctive carved doors at the Inn of the Anasazi near the plaza are inspired by various traditions, including Pueblo imagery, Hispanic chip-carving, and art deco silhouettes, creating a progressive Pueblo deco expression. (Courtesy Jeremy Morrelli)*

*135. FLATHEADS, ceramic sculpture, K. D. Fullerton. Fullerton's inventive ceramic art recalls the forms and imagery of early Anasazi religious icons. (Courtesy K. D. Fullerton)*

*136. James Jareb House, interior, Santa Fe. In designer James Jareb's world, northern Africa and northern New Mexico are linked by spirit and art. Jareb's own house/studio/gallery reflects his philosophy of art and life. The house's interiors are a marriage of "Santa Fe" and North African design concepts, and the rooms resonate with an almost mystical energy. (Courtesy James Jareb)*

that is available to the public. Many do-it-yourself home builders in the Santa Fe area are taking advantage of the opportunity.

New Mexican music has benefited from a worldwide explosion of postmodernist expressions in Spanish and Latin American music. The European-based group the Gipsy Kings has become an international musical sensation with music that is an amalgamation of traditional Spanish flamenco music, Moorish and jazz elements, and even popular lounge classics such as "Volare." The Chilean musical ensemble Inti-Illimani fuses traditional Latin American folk music with other contemporary international styles. Santa Fe is a natural hotbed for postmodern Spanish and Latin American music, and local performers such as internationally acclaimed guitarist Ottmar Liebert add a personal touch to Spanish flamenco.

New Mexican cuisine has evolved from a basic subsistence diet of corn, chile, beans, and squash to a highly sophisticated, bold, and inventive menu. Led by master chef and food entrepreneur Mark Miller of Santa Fe's Coyote Cafe, chefs throughout the Southwest and across the country are currently offering "Nouvelle Mexique" cuisine.

Traditional ingredients of southwestern, American, and continental cooking are being combined in imaginative ways. Never before have so many varieties of chiles been served on southwestern plates. Lobster enchiladas, chipotle shrimp, Yucatán lamb with smoked chile sauce, and red chile onion rings are just a few of the tantalizing entrées offered by Miller at the Coyote Cafe. In 1992, Red Sage, Miller's southwestern restaurant in Washington, D. C., was named "Restaurant of the Year" by *Esquire*.

Nouvelle Mexique cuisine has also spawned a separate agricultural industry—a revival in the growing of ancient foods such as Anasazi beans, various strains of corn, and other prehistoric vegetables that were long ago lost to the southwestern dinner table.

137. *Buffalo* trastero, *L. D. Burke III. Burke employs the familiar Hispanic upright chest, or* trastero, *as a canvas for his classic western theme of buffalo on the open range. (Courtesy L. D. Burke III Furniture)*

138. *L. D. Burke's colorful cowboy-style furniture expresses the postmodern design attitude of witty takeoffs on historical tradition. (Courtesy L. D. Burke III Furniture)*

139. *Navajo chief chair, Jeremy Morrelli. Master carver and designer Jeremy Morrelli marries simple Navajo designs with art deco profiling and Chippendale proportions to create a modern furniture classic. (Courtesy Morrelli Furniture)*

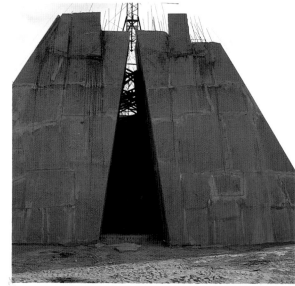

140. *(Opposite page, top)* STAR AXIS, *stone and earthwork, Charles Ross. Artist Charles Ross began excavation and construction of Star Axis near Las Vegas, New Mexico. A monumental sculpture scientifically designed as an observatory, it is eleven stories high and spans one-tenth of a mile. A 200-foot star tunnel (top left), which forms the core of the sculpture, is aligned with the earth's axis and offers unique viewing of Polaris, the North Star, including past and future simulations. The 50-foot pyramid below the tunnel (top right and lower right), is oriented to the sun and marks its angle at the solstices. The observatory is scheduled to be completed and open to the public in 1996. (Photograph by Marcia Keegan)*

141. *(Opposite page, bottom) The Douglas Johnson House, work in progress designed and built by Douglas Johnson. The artist has drawn inspiration from the designs and techniques of the ancient pueblo builders. Exterior (lower left): Johnson has incorporated natural rock formations into the structure, and the walls are subtly ornamented with banded stonework. (Photograph by Marcia Keegan). Interior (lower right): The rock formation creates a dominating sculptural wall. The ceiling, constructed of natural woods in a simple formal pattern, complements the stone and rock walls with warmth and symmetry. (Photograph by Marcia Keegan)*

142. CRUCIFIX, *Tony Price. Since 1965, New Mexico sculptor Tony Price has been creating icons of the world's religions out of scrap materials from Los Alamos National Laboratory. (Photograph by Marcia Keegan)*

143. *Indigenous American harvest. Seeds of Change is a biodiversity company, pioneering the sale of organically grown seeds for backyard farmers. The company has also worked closely with native people to preserve ancient agricultural techniques. American vegetables are being carefully cultivated and crossbred as seen in this harvest display. (Courtesy Seeds of Change)*

144. *Zuñi waffle gardens, 1911. The ingenious Zuñi Pueblo waffle gardens maximize the use of precious water in the desert Southwest. (Photograph by Jesse Nusbaum, Museum of New Mexico Photo Archives, Santa Fe, Neg. No. 43170)*

Zuñi Pueblo has undertaken a remarkable economic development project to recultivate the pueblo's own traditional plants from ancient seeds stored in seed jars for centuries. Zuñi's famous "waffle gardens," among the most efficient gardening systems known, are also being reconstructed.

Traditional New Mexican cooking, differentiated from Tex-Mex, Mexican, and California Mexican by the use of long, savory New Mexican chile peppers, is as popular as ever. Mexican or southwestern food is perhaps America's fastest growing cuisine (more salsa than ketchup is now sold). But only within the past ten years, within the postmodern era, has the true potential of the southwestern menu begun to be realized.

The New Age or spiritual frontier can also be said to be in a postmodern mode. Many people no longer follow orthodox religious teachings, but combine prayer and meditation techniques from a variety of sources. "Synthesis," even in the case of religious experience, seems to be a buzzword for the 1990s.

Traditional religions, such as Christianity, Buddhism, Judaism, Hinduism, Islam, and Native American faiths, continue to thrive in the Southwest, but a variety of alternative forms of spirituality are also available. In Santa Fe, solutions to the problems of living may be sought and found through psychotherapy, physical therapy, psychic investigation, or philosophical studies. In other words, challenging and exciting spiritual opportunities are offered.

Environmentalists have always been attracted to New Mexico. The pristine landscapes, rugged sculpted earth, immense skies, and unusual vegetation are potent arguments for environmental protection rather than exploitation. Tutored by the land's original inhabitants, many people now espouse a "Native American" reverence for the land, for Mother

Earth, and perhaps this reverence could become the seed of our planet's survival.

The amazing Santa Fe boom and the postmodern Santa Fe fantasy continue unabated in the 1990s. A true lifestyle frontier in New Mexico has spontaneously evolved over many centuries, but this evolution has been greatly accelerated over the past few years by the extraordinary global attention focused on the region and also by a massive and unprecedented immigration of highly talented and globally conscious people.

This southwestern paradise has a dark lining, however, not unlike that experienced by other golden cities such as Venice and San Francisco. Development pressures are altering the legendary landscapes and displacing native residents from their homes. Many people claim that Santa Fe is already a caricature of itself—an adobe Disneyland.

Historically, New Mexico and its people have displayed a remarkable cultural tenacity and ability to absorb change and the influences of the outside world. In the "Land of Poco Tiempo," time, people, and events are slowed down to a reasonable and civilized pace. The Pueblo Indians learned this patience long ago, and hopefully so shall the rest of us.

*145.* SPIRIT LADDERS OVER TAOS PUEBLO, *watercolor, by Carol Bowles. The actual architecture and landscape become a stylized unity in Bowles' paintings, with people and animals as secondary actors in the cosmic drama of the ceremonial and everyday life of Pueblo Indians. (Courtesy Carol Bowles)*

*146.* DID I TELL YOU I LOVE YOU?, *oil on canvas, by Bernadette Vigil. Bernadette Vigil draws on romantic and spiritual themes in this painting. In New Mexico, traditional cultures embody qualities of love, reverence for the land, and a belief in the benevolent mystical power of a supernatural realm. (Courtesy Owings-Dewey Fine Art, Santa Fe)*

# $\mathcal{E}$PILOGUE

Nearly two thousand years of myth and legend have combined to help create the Santa Fe fantasy. Mythical kingdoms of wealth in the West lured explorers ever onward.

The medieval myth of the Seven Cities of Antilia, rumored to lie in the Western Sea, became transformed into the myth of the Seven Golden Cities of Cíbola in the early sixteenth century. Cíbola and its gold attracted Coronado's expeditionary army northward in 1540, initiating a series of migrations to New Mexico, migrations that successfully used the Santa Fe Trail (1821–1879), the Santa Fe Railroad (1880–1920), and Route 66 (1926–1974).

Though the fantasy of gold in the Southwest long ago perished, other forms of wealth were discovered in New Mexico in the twentieth century. Traditional Native American and Hispanic cultures, pristine dramatic landscapes, an elusive quality of magic in the air and light, a latent power and spirituality in the land—these are the enduring treasures of Santa Fe and New Mexico.

As the global and spiritual consciousness of mankind has matured over the past two millenia, many people have forsaken the pursuit of gold and riches in favor of other types of rewards. Global politics in the 1990s and beyond seem destined to include serious discussions of environmental protection and energy conserva-

tion. Healthy diets and stress-free lifestyles will continue to be promoted. Santa Fe promises to play an important role in the ongoing project of saving our planet and creating a better life for its inhabitants.

As if by an alchemist's wand, the Santa Fe fantasy has been transformed over time into the pursuit of a personal utopia. Spiritual transcendence, living in harmony with the land, and the development of personal artistic and cutural expression are among the treasures being sought in the mountains of northern New Mexico. The appeal of the Santa Fe fantasy is stronger now than ever before.

147. FOLK ART COLLECTORS, *wood and paint*, bulto *by Luis Tapia. Luis Tapia's gift of incisive social satire is apparent in this* bulto *of Santa Fe tourists displaying the icons of their avocation. (Collection of Lynn Steiner; courtesy Owings-Dewey Fine Art, Santa Fe)*

148. ORIOLES, *casein, by Douglas Johnson. A pastoral paradise in the mountains of northern New Mexico is the goal of many modern "Santa Fe fantasies." (Courtesy the Gerald Peters Gallery, Santa Fe)*

149. *Arthur Medina's lowrider, Chimayó, New Mexico. Customizing cars with chrome, hydraulic suspension systems, and meticulous paint jobs is recognized as a popular art form in New Mexico. Known as "lowriders," these cars are proud symbols of modern Hispanic culture in New Mexico. (Photograph by Marcia Keegan)*